Political Advertising in the United States

Political Advertising in the United States

Erika Franklin Fowler
Wesleyan University

Michael M. Franz
Bowdoin College

Travis N. Ridout
Washington State University

Co-directors of the Wesleyan Media Project

WESTVIEW
PRESS

A Member of the Perseus Books Group

Westview Press was founded in 1975 in Boulder, Colorado, by notable publisher and intellectual Fred Praeger. Westview Press continues to publish scholarly titles and high-quality undergraduate- and graduate-level textbooks in core social science disciplines. With books developed, written, and edited with the needs of serious nonfiction readers, professors, and students in mind, Westview Press honors its long history of publishing books that matter.

Copyright © 2016 by Westview Press
Published by Westview Press,
A Member of the Perseus Books Group
2465 Central Avenue
Boulder, CO 80301
www.westviewpress.com

Westview Press books are available at special discounts for bulk purchases in the United States by corporations, institutions, and other organizations. For more information, please contact the Special Markets Department at the Perseus Books Group, 2300 Chestnut Street, Suite 200, Philadelphia, PA 19103, or call (800) 810-4145, ext. 5000, or e-mail special.markets@perseusbooks.com.

Library of Congress Cataloging-in-Publication Data

Names: Fowler, Erika Franklin, author. | Franz, Michael M., 1976- author. |
    Ridout, Travis N., 1974- author.
Title: Political advertising in the United States / Erika Franklin Fowler,
    Wesleyan University ; Michael M. Franz, Bowdoin College ; Travis N.
    Ridout, Washington State University.
Description: Boulder, CO : Westview Press, 2016. | Includes bibliographical
    references and index.
Identifiers: LCCN 2015036822| ISBN 9780813349756 (paperback) | ISBN
    9780813350103 (e-book)
Subjects: LCSH: Advertising, Political--United States. | Television in
    politics--United States. | Political campaigns--United States. | BISAC:
    POLITICAL SCIENCE / Political Process / Elections. | SOCIAL SCIENCE /
    Media Studies.
Classification: LCC JF2112.A4 F68 2016 | DDC 324.7/30973--dc23 LC record available at http://lccn.loc.gov/2015036822

10 9 8 7 6 5 4 3 2 1

Contents

List of Illustrations

Preface

This book has its roots in North Hall at the University of Wisconsin, Madison, where we were all graduate students and research assistants working with Wisconsin Advertising Project data for Ken Goldstein. As professors now ourselves and directors of the Wesleyan Media Project (which has taken over where the Wisconsin Advertising Project left off), we spend a lot of time watching, researching, and writing about political advertising. We also frequently talk to students, journalists, and interested citizens about trends in advertising and what we know about its influence. Some of what we present in this book is intuitive to our audiences (for instance, that campaigns are more negative now than they were a decade ago), and some of it is not (for instance, that negative ads play an important role in educating political novices). Fundamentally, we—both individually and as directors of the Wesleyan Media Project—are driven by a desire to provide the public with information about the content and influence of political advertising and how it is changing. This book represents one more way to do just that.

Collectively, we have spent nearly forty-five years analyzing political ads, and we aren't sick of them yet. In fact, quite the opposite. Despite the thousands of ads we've viewed and the millions of airings we've analyzed, every election cycle brings new tactics and new trends to examine, and we are always excited to see what pops up as we conduct our real-time analyses. Many of the patterns in advertising are predictable, but campaigns are constantly innovating, and of course, each year brings different candidates, themes, and groups to the table.

In addition, since our days in Wisconsin, a lot has changed in technology, ad targeting, and the campaign finance regulations that govern advertising on television. And those changes have consequences.

Television advertising is still the primary mechanism through which campaigns talk to the majority of citizens, and it remains the most visible manifestation of a campaign season. We don't see that changing in the immediate future, but we are seeing changes in who is sponsoring ads, and this may have important consequences for citizens. Recent court decisions have created a campaign finance environment that encourages and emboldens interest group activity in elections. This may make it difficult for voters to hold those ad sponsors accountable for what they say: how do you punish a group for the attack ads it airs when that "group" is no more than a bare-bones legal entity?

At the same time, campaigns are getting increasingly sophisticated in how they target advertising, thanks, in part, to their ability to access so much data about each and every one of us. Because of this, future campaigns may see television advertising deployed in ways similar to online ads—directed toward specific individuals with specific characteristics.

Changes in technology have also facilitated this targeting of specific individuals. Campaigns can now more precisely locate the types of voters they want to speak to by turning to national or local cable television—or by moving to online advertising. Increased targeting means fewer "accidental" exposures to advertising, which may actually decrease the amount of knowledge about candidates and issues that advertising imparts to the larger population. It also means that campaigns increasingly may be about "nothing," as the campaign you experience may be a much different one than the campaign your neighbor experiences.

In spite of these changes, we are convinced that televised political advertising is not rapidly approaching extinction. Rather, it will remain an important part—though not the only part—of a campaign's message strategy.

With a project of this size, we have acquired numerous debts. In a very real sense, this book would not exist without Ken Goldstein. With him as professor, mentor, and friend, we have benefitted enormously from his guidance and are indebted to him for having faith in us to pick up the ad tracking mantle with the creation of the Wesleyan Media Project. We are enormously grateful for the tireless work of our project manager, Laura Baum, the research associates (Katie Searles, Jenny Holland, Laci Hubbard-Mattix, and Orion Yoesle), the coding supervisors (Matt Motta, Justin Pottle, Olivia Horton, Michael Linden, and Eliza Loomis), and the cadre of student researchers who have made our real-time tracking possible, especially Alex Hunt, Emma Lewis, Leo Liu, Marshal Lawler, Ross Petchler, Sam Savitch, David Shor, Rachel Warren, Zach Wulderk, Rachel Ellman, and Michael Yoshida, as well as numerous others. We thank James Fowler and CommIT Technology for the website and online analysis system that facilitates our coding across institutions. Thank you to Kris McQueeney for administrative support. We also thank Manolis Kaparakis and Wesleyan's Quantitative Analysis Center (QAC), Lauren Rubenstein and Wesleyan's Office of University Communications along with Heather Tolley-Bauer for PR pinch-hitting in 2012, and Carolyn Kaufman, Rose Pandolfo, and Carol Scully in Wesleyan's Office of Corporate, Foundation and Government Grants for all of their support. We thank the Center for Responsive Politics for a productive partnership. Funding for the Wesleyan Media Project has come from The John S. and James L. Knight Foundation, The John D. and Catherine T. MacArthur Foundation, Sunlight Foundation, Rockefeller Brothers Fund, Bowdoin College, Washington State University, and Wesleyan University. We are especially grateful to Wesleyan and to several Wesleyan deans and administrators who deserve thanks for their ongoing support of the project, including Don Moon, Joe Bruno, Gary Shaw, Rob Rosenthal, Marc Eisner, Joyce Jacobsen, Ruth Striegel Weissman, Charles Salas, and Michael Roth.

The advisory board for the Wesleyan Media Project also deserves kudos. Thanks to John Geer, Keena Lipsitz, Peter Overby, Charlie

Mahtesian, Matea Gold, Daniela Altimari, and Fredreka Schouten for their incredible insights and advice.

We are grateful to Ada Fung, our Westview Press editor, for her guidance and helpful feedback throughout the process. Many thanks to the rest of the Westview team, especially Managing Assistant Editor Krista Anderson, Sales and Marketing Director Renee Legatt, Senior Sales Manager Victoria Henson, our project editor, Carolyn Sobczak, and our copyeditor, Erin Granville, for their hard work on the book. We would also like to thank the peer reviewers for their detailed and thoughtful feedback on the manuscript, including: Todd Belt (University of Hawai'i at Hilo); Julio Borquez (University of Michigan, Dearborn); Johanna Dunaway (Louisiana State University); Matthew Eshbaugh-Soha (University of North Texas); Mark Glantz (St. Norbert College); Alison Howard (Dominican University of California); Diana Owen (Georgetown University); Laurie Rhodebeck (University of Louisville); John Barry Ryan (Florida State University); Edward Sidlow (Eastern Michigan University); and others who wished to remain anonymous.

We are indebted to our families for their unfailing support through all of the real-time tracking craziness and never-ending manuscript writing. To James, Laura, and Carolyn, words cannot express our gratitude, and to William, Charles, Charlie, Henry, Lorelei, Julianne, and Isaac, who provide daily joy and inspiration, we are forever grateful.

Erika Franklin Fowler
Michael M. Franz
Travis N. Ridout

CHAPTER 1

Introduction

Pretend for the moment that it is November 1, 2012, just a few days before Election Day, and you are living in Richmond, Virginia. After a long day, you return to your apartment ready for some relaxation. You turn on some mindless television, specifically, *Entertainment Tonight* on Channel 12, which is Richmond's NBC affiliate. At 5:09 p.m., an ad from the Romney campaign comes on. This is followed thirty seconds later by an ad from the National Republican Senatorial Committee promoting Senate candidate George Allen. This ad is then followed immediately by an ad sponsored by the Democratic Senatorial Campaign Committee promoting Allen's opponent, Tim Kaine. Thirty seconds later, an ad sponsored by Priorities USA Action, President Obama's super PAC, appears on your television screen. The celebrity gossip on *Entertainment Tonight* resumes for a few minutes, but at 5:14 p.m., the political ads return. In this commercial break, you see three ads: one sponsored by Obama's campaign; one sponsored by the campaign of House member Eric Cantor; and one attacking both Obama and Kaine that's sponsored by Crossroads GPS, an outside group. During the program's last commercial break at 5:25 p.m., you see three more political ads. Just thirty minutes of watching television and you've already seen five minutes' worth of political ads. That's as much, if not more, politics as you would have seen had you watched the local news for half an hour. And imagine if you had watched Channel 12 all day long. You would have seen 258 political ads, for a grand total of two hours and nine minutes' worth of campaign messages in one day!

Those thirty minutes of television in Richmond, Virginia, help illustrate some important points about political advertising. The first is the ubiquity of televised political advertising close to an election. Richmond is a fairly typical **media market**, a region in which the population receives similar television and radio stations. Nine hundred political ads for presidential, Senate, or House candidates were aired on Richmond's five broadcast television stations on November 1, but Richmond was not even in the top ten media markets that day in terms of the number of ads aired. In fact, Richmond was tied for twenty-eight.

Let's look at the period between January 1, 2012, and Election Day, November 6, and expand our scope from Richmond to all 210 media markets in the United States. Table 1.1 shows the number of ad airings (sometimes called **spots**) on broadcast television, national network television, and national cable television in three different types of races. In races for the US House, almost 700,000 spots aired across the country, at an estimated cost of $428 million. For the Senate, it was 925,000 spots at a cost of $545 million. Advertising was even more intense in the presidential race, with 1.4 million spots aired at an estimated cost of $950 million. All told, over three million spots were aired in federal races in 2012, at a cost of almost two billion dollars. If you add in spots aired on behalf of candidates for governor, state representative, country coroner, and other elected positions (our data include any ad for elected office that aired on local broadcast stations), the cost of all spots aired in 2012 reaches over three and a half billion dollars, accounting for over four million airings.

Second, the Richmond example also illustrates the diversity of advertising sponsors. There were ads paid for by the candidates' campaigns, the political parties, and a variety of outside groups, including **501c organizations,** like Crossroads GPS, and **super PACs,** like Priorities USA Action. Organizations carrying the 501c designation are defined in the tax code as non-profits, which allows them to raise unlimited amounts of money from individual donors and spend

Table 1.1: Ads Aired in Federal Races in 2012 and Estimated Costs

Race	Number of Spots	Est. Cost
House	685,787	$428M
Senate	925,135	$545M
President	1,431,939	$950M
	3,042,861	$1.9B

Source: Wesleyan Media Project.

that money on ads, and they are not required to disclose publicly the names of the donors. Super PACs can also raise and spend unlimited amounts, but they must make public all expenditures and donors.

Not all that long ago, the candidates' official campaigns paid for most of the ads aired on their behalf, but that is no longer the case in many races. To give just one example, in the general election presidential race in 2012, outside groups collectively aired more advertisements supporting Mitt Romney than did the Romney campaign. As a result of this movement toward outside group advertisers, some wonder: do campaigns control their own messages, or are they at the mercy of big-dollar groups with agendas of their own? We will discuss this more in Chapter 9.

Third, the Richmond example looks at ads aired during *Entertainment Tonight* to highlight the fact that political advertising isn't shown only during political programs (such as political talks shows or twenty-four-hour news channels), and important information about candidates for office doesn't appear solely on those shows. On the contrary, campaigns frequently place advertisements on nonpolitical television shows to reach key audiences that are not predisposed to pay much attention to public affairs. Although people have lots of programming choices when they turn on their television sets, they have a hard time avoiding political advertisements no matter what they watch—especially in markets with competitive races—due to the sheer volume of ads on the airwaves. Furthermore, campaigns are becoming increasingly sophisticated at targeting advertising messages to the types of audiences they believe are tuning in to particular programs.

WHY STUDY POLITICAL ADVERTISING?

Televised political advertising—and that's what the term *political advertising* refers to throughout most of this book—is the primary way candidates attempt to reach voters and thus is the most visible part of the campaign for many voters. Certainly there are other ways campaigns try to communicate with voters and the news media, but television advertising continues to comprise the largest share of many campaign budgets. Furthermore, creative content and campaign messages are designed, first and foremost, with television advertising in mind. Thus, understanding political campaigns requires understanding how political advertising is created and deployed, and how developments in technology and the regulatory environment have shaped campaigns' choices and their ability to speak directly to voters. Of course, all of these decisions and changes have implications for how advertising influences the electorate. For these reasons, any in-depth examination of modern political campaigning must include an understanding of the creation, strategic deployment, and influence of political advertising.

FOUR KEY ARGUMENTS

In this book, we will advance four main arguments about political advertising.

1. The regulatory environment has had a huge impact on the sponsorship and content of political ads. Since 2007, there has been a string of US Supreme Court rulings and rule changes by the **Federal Election Commission (FEC)**, the government agency that regulates the financing of federal campaigns, that have had a major impact on how easy it is for an outside group to become involved in a political advertising campaign. In brief, these changes in the regulatory environment have made it much easier for outside groups to raise money for television advertising and for these groups to expressly endorse a candidate. Any ad sponsor can now urge viewers to "Vote for Barack Obama" or "Vote for Mitt Romney." In the past, interest groups hoping to be this explicit had to raise their money in highly regulated ways. Chapter 2 will provide the details of these changes, but one important result is the increased presence of big-money donors funding big-money interest groups.

2. *"Big data" has led to increasingly sophisticated ad targeting.* In the 2004 campaign, the Republican Party began placing its advertisements on certain television programs in order to get more bang for their buck. They knew, based on massive consumer surveys, which programs Democrats, Republicans, and persuadable voters watched, and they knew whether the audience of each program was likely or unlikely to vote. For example, if you want to speak to Democrats who are almost certain to vote, you should advertise during *60 Minutes*. The audience for *The Simpsons* is also heavily Democratic, but it contains a lot of people who are unlikely to vote. If you want to find a lot of Republican voters, then advertising during sports is a good bet, especially college football on Saturday nights or *Sunday Night Football*.[1] The audiences for programs such as *The Big Bang Theory, The Mentalist,* and *NCIS* all skew Republican, while those for programs such as *Saturday Night Live, Project Runway,* and *Antiques Roadshow* are highly Democratic.[2] More recently, campaigns have started using data on people's television viewing habits obtained from cable set-top boxes. These data on household viewing habits have been matched to databases containing information on millions of consumers, which allows campaigns to reach very specific categories of voters with their messages. Chapter 5 provides much more detail on how this targeting takes place.

3. *Recent technological advances have increased the efficiency of ad distribution.* Traditionally, campaigns could place their ads on national and local broadcast television. Local television has the advantage of allowing campaigns to target their messages geographically. But now cable television allows campaigns to reach niche audiences across multiple markets, such as highly knowledgeable Republicans

watching Fox News, women watching Lifetime or Hallmark Channel, or parents watching Nick Jr. with their children. Moreover, the recent growth of **cable interconnects**—groups of local cable television systems that are linked together—allows cable companies to easily insert ads between programs, and those ads can be targeted to certain cities or even neighborhoods. This helps campaigns to spend their money efficiently; they don't waste money on ads that will be seen by people who live outside the electoral district or who are unlikely to support the candidate. Finally, campaigns now have the capacity to buy online ads that appear only in geographic locations or on websites where they are likely to reach a receptive audience. Chapters 5 and 6 discuss how these technological changes have made advertising more efficient.

4. All of these developments have influenced the persuasive impact of ads. The increase in dollars going to advertising as a result of the new regulatory environment means that people are seeing more ads than ever before. But more important for gauging the impact of advertising on who wins an election is that, thanks to better ad targeting and distribution, voters are increasingly being exposed to unbalanced message flows. It is no longer the case that for each Republican ad you see, you also see one Democratic ad. If someone decides to anonymously back the Democratic candidate through a ten-million-dollar donation to a group supporting that candidate, then you may see four Democratic ads for each Republican ad. And depending on the television stations and programs you watch and the websites you visit, you may see eight Democratic ads for each Republican ad due to targeting. Increasingly common unbalanced message flows like these make voter persuasion and mobilization more likely. Chapter 7 examines this role of advertising in persuading people to vote in a certain way.

HISTORY OF CAMPAIGN ADVERTISING

Before we delve deeper into the issues noted above, let's take a quick look at the history of campaign ads in the US for some context of what has and hasn't changed in the political advertising landscape. Televised political advertising has been around for over sixty years.

Scholars believe that the first campaign ad in the United States was aired in 1950 by Senator William Benton of Connecticut, who had a career as an ad executive. The first presidential campaign ads appeared on American televisions in 1952, a year in which about a third of American households had televisions.[3] This series of ads, each of which was twenty seconds in length, was aired by Dwight Eisenhower's presidential campaign. Each featured an ordinary voter asking Eisenhower a question and Eisenhower's quick response. Production value was low: there was no music, and both the citizen and Eisenhower were seen in front of a grey background. That same year, Eisenhower also ran an ad with cartoon animation showing a parade of people (and an elephant) carrying "Ike" signs. (See Figure 1.1.) These images were accompanied by a catchy jingle ("I like Ike"), but there was no discussion of policy. Eisenhower's Democratic opponent, Adlai Stevenson, aired an ad with a woman singing a song that mentions Stevenson's Illinois roots and experience as a soldier.

By 1956, some political ads already were negative. One ad sponsored by Adlai Stevenson—once again the Democratic nominee—showed a clip of Eisenhower calling for the return of "integrity and thrift" to Washington. The ad then transitioned to Senator Estes Kefauver, the Democrats' vice-presidential nominee, calling it "another promise the general didn't keep." By 1964, negative ads not only called out opponents but also created a dark and angst-filled mood. One ad sponsored by President Lyndon Johnson that attacked his Republican opponent, Barry Goldwater, featured video of Ku Klux Klan members burning a cross at nighttime. The voiceover announcer then quoted a member of the Alabama Klan saying, "I like Barry Goldwater. He needs our help." Other Johnson ads raised the possibility of atomic war were Goldwater to be elected. One used a quote in which Goldwater called the atomic bomb "merely another weapon." Another showed a girl licking an ice cream cone while the female narrator talked about the "strontium-90" and "cesium-137" from atomic bombs that "can make you die." The punch line, of course, was that Goldwater wanted to continue testing such atomic bombs. The idea that politics in the United States was quite tame in the 1950s and early 1960s is challenged by the content of these ads.

Figure 1.1: Eisenhower's "I Like Ike" Ad from 1952

Source: Video courtesy of the Dwight D. Eisenhower Presidential Library

By 1968, televised presidential campaign ads were in color. Republican Richard Nixon deployed ads with upsetting, dissonant music and images of protesters, burning buildings, people injecting drugs, and soldiers in combat in Vietnam. Democrat Hubert Humphrey tried to connect with voters by releasing an ad that showed him, dressed casually, chatting informally with citizens while sitting on a dock on a lake. Many ads that year were a minute in length, but by 1976, thirty-second ads were becoming much more common; many ads looked similar to the ads that we see on television today.

What has changed since the 1970s? For one, the sponsorship of advertising. We will see in Chapter 3 that, thanks to both changes in campaign finance rules and Supreme Court decisions, interest groups are now taking a much more prominent role in paying for advertising. A second shift is in the tone of advertising. Although negative ads are nothing new, they are much more common now than they were in the first few decades of political advertising in the United States. A third change is in where ads are aired. Through the 1980s, many presidential ads were aired on national television networks, but by the 1990s, almost all advertising had moved to local broadcast television. More recently, advertising has been moving to national and local cable, enabling better targeting of desired voters. Finally, although television remains dominant, campaigns have made more use of online-only advertising in the past few election cycles. This has allowed them to experiment with content and develop new ad formats. We discuss ad targeting on television in Chapter 5 and online ads in Chapter 6.

TRACKING TELEVISION ADVERTISING

How can we know so much about how many television ads aired in recent campaigns and what these ads were about? We are fortunate to direct the Wesleyan Media Project (WMP), an enterprise that has tracked and analyzed all television ads airing on broadcast and national cable outlets in all 210 media markets in the United States since 2010. As graduate students, we were employed by the Wisconsin Advertising Project, which tracked a slightly more limited set of advertisements between 1998 and 2008. The underlying data for our analysis comes from a commercial company, Kantar Media/CMAG, which provides us with two important data sources. The first is a comprehensive database containing information including the market, station, date, and exact time of each airing, in addition to the program on which each ad aired and an estimate of the cost the sponsor was likely to have paid. The second is a video of each ad aired.

A team of trained students watches each video and compiles additional information about each ad's content. For example, we research the entity responsible for airing each ad, distinguishing between candidate-sponsored ads and those sponsored by parties or interest groups. We further classify ads into three categories: (1) positive (or promotional) ads that talk solely about the favored candidate; (2) purely negative (or attack) ads that, save for the "paid for by" line (for instance, "I'm Barack Obama, and I approve this message"), talk solely about the opponent; and (3) contrast (or comparative) ads, which contain information about both candidates. In addition, we keep track of whether an ad references other national politicians or party leaders, whether the favored candidate or opponent appears in the ad, and what types of references are used about the candidates (for instance, if the candidate or opponent is described as honest or dishonest). We also track which issues are mentioned in an ad, such as terrorism, gun control, or the economy.

PLAN OF THE BOOK

Chapter 2 starts by taking you back to the 1970s to describe how the financing of campaigns and advertising was first regulated by the government and then traces how those regulations have changed. To demonstrate the impact of those changes—and to give you a flavor of how advertising is deployed in the current era—Chapter 3 provides you with detailed data on the volume and content of advertising in recent campaigns. Chapter 4 gets into the nitty-gritty of how ads are created, while Chapter 5 discusses the options for disseminating ads and how those options are used to target specific groups of voters. Chapter 6 describes the role of online advertising, how it compares to traditional television advertising, and the different ways in which it is deployed. Chapters 7 and 8 explore how political advertising affects voters—not only the decisions that they make but their propensity to participate in politics and their attitudes toward the political system. Our final chapter considers the role of advertising in contemporary American election campaigns and makes an argument that you may not expect: Although citizens may grow sick of the thirty-second ads they see on televisions screens each campaign season, these ads are not

inherently bad. They may, in fact, serve a positive purpose by informing and engaging the electorate.

DISCUSSION QUESTIONS

1. What comes to mind when you think of political advertising?
   What components of an ad stick out to you?
2. Think about a recent candidate for office. How did you hear
   about him or her? Did you learn any of the information you
   know about him or her through a political advertisement?
3. Why is understanding the use of political advertising in the
   United States important? Is it less important to understand in
   other countries? If yes, why?
4. Think about the most recent presidential campaign. Which ad
   that aired during that campaign comes to mind first? Why is it
   so memorable?

NOTES

1. National Media, *2010 Media Buying Trends: Part 2,* http://www.natmedia
.com/2012/02/03/2010-media-buying-trends-primetime-tv-part-2/.

2. James Hibberd, "Republicans vs. Democrats Favorite TV Shows Revealed,"
EW.com, November 3, 2014, http://www.ew.com/article/2014/11/03/republican
-democrats-favorite-tv-shows.

3. Markus Prior, *Post-Broadcast Democracy: How Media Choice Increases Inequality in Political Involvement and Polarizes Elections* (New York: Cambridge
University Press, 2007), 16.

CHAPTER 2

The Regulation of Advertising

To conceive, test, produce, and air campaign advertising costs money. Because of this, ad sponsors have to commit a considerable amount of time and energy to raising money. This is the first and most immediate task of any candidate for federal office. This is also true for the party committees that seek to promote and elect their candidates and for the interest groups that align with a candidate or promote their policies and issues during a campaign. The time and energy needed to amass a media budget, however, are not equal for all political advertisers. Fund-raising efforts are guided by campaign finance rules, but candidates face one set of rules while parties must abide by another, slightly different set, and interest groups follow yet another set of rules. Most importantly, these rules have changed and shifted over time. Demonstrating these shifts is one of the primary goals of this chapter.

The rules are only part of the story, however. The way the rules shape political behavior is equally important. In this chapter, we review a number of trends in political advertising that are influenced by campaign finance rules. First, fund-raising and advertising are intricately linked. Because candidates devote so much of their war chests to advertising, they are forced to raise ever more funds to compete with their opponents. Second, party and interest-group ad sponsors pay a lot more for airtime than candidates do, a direct consequence of the way campaign finance rules are written. To the extent that these sponsors become more numerous—an unquestionable reality of recent elections—the cost of campaigns increases. Finally, while parties and candidates must be completely transparent in the disclosure of their contributors, many prominent and high-profile interest groups are not similarly legally required to reveal their donor base. This allows a whole host of political contributors to remain in the shadows.

No single chapter can do justice to the dynamic and varied laws and judicial decisions that pertain to campaign finance. What we outline here, more modestly, are the broad parameters of campaign finance law. Our goal is to demonstrate that the rules matter and that they determine how ad sponsors raise and spend money. In fact, understanding these rules is critical to understanding some of the major trends in political advertising over the last twenty years.

THE RULES OF CAMPAIGN FINANCING

Congress passed a major campaign finance reform bill, the **Federal Election Campaign Act (FECA)**, in 1971 and revised and expanded it in 1974. These reforms were the first major and comprehensive updates of campaign finance in nearly sixty years.[1] The 1971 reforms were actually more modest than the 1974 changes, which were primarily reactions to the Watergate controversy that engulfed the Nixon presidency between 1972 and 1974. The Supreme Court invalidated some of the 1974 laws in 1976 in a case called **Buckley v. Valeo**, and Congress responded soon after with further revisions to reflect the court's mandates. These developments, largely complete by 1976, set up the system as we know it today.

Candidates

FECA and the revisions made to it throughout the 1970s dictate that candidates are expressly banned from accepting direct contributions from corporations and unions and may accept contributions from only three sources: individual citizens, party committees, and **political action committees (PACs)**.[2] PACs are associations of individuals affiliated with corporations, unions, or trade associations. Members of PACs—and there are strict rules for what constitutes membership in a PAC—pool their own money into a common pot, which is then distributed to candidates as the leaders of the PAC see fit.[3] Corporate executives and holders of corporate stock can give to a corporation's PAC from their own paycheck, and labor PACs raise money from the rank and file in the union. PACs are often vilified as "special interests," but all of the money PACs contribute to candidate coffers comes from the voluntary contributions of PAC members. It is not inaccurate to say that every penny collected by candidates is, at its true source, a personal contribution from citizen bank accounts.

Moreover, contributions are strictly limited in size. FECA capped party and PAC contributions to candidates at five thousand dollars per election—a limit that has remained in effect for forty years—and individual contributions at one thousand dollars per election. In 2002, the limit on individual contributions was doubled to two thousand dollars and indexed to inflation, so that in 2014, an individual could give $2,600 to a candidate per election. This limit applies to us the authors, to you the readers, and to the millionaires and billionaires who might prefer to flex their financial muscle a bit more in electoral politics.

Candidates in contemporary federal elections do not have it easy when it comes to raising the funds needed to run for election or reelection. To be sure, incumbents have a deep network of existing supporters and access to many PACs in the nation's capital,[4] but one would be hard-pressed to find even one incumbent member of Congress who would argue that the current rules of campaign finance make running for office easy.

It is also vital to consider the limits that the reform efforts of the 1970s placed on candidate spending. Expenditure limits had been a goal of campaign finance reform efforts as far back as the early twentieth century, and in 1971 and 1974 Congress placed restrictions on total candidate expenditures generally and on candidate ad spending specifically. For example, the 1974 law limited House candidates in states with more than one district to spending only seventy thousand dollars in a primary or general election. The 1971 law capped candidates' media expenditures: federal candidates could spend only 60 percent of their overall budget on television and radio advertising.[5] It is remarkable to think that Congress had the votes in 1971 and 1974 to establish these sorts of hard limits on media spending.

Congressional limits on candidate media spending were hardly in place long enough to matter, though. All but the contribution limits were overturned in *Buckley*. The justices reasoned that election spending is equivalent to election speech, and so placing any limit on how much candidates can spend to run for office—or to spread their message via television and radio—was a direct limitation on what and how much candidates can say.

This is no small matter. The First Amendment is clear that Congress has no constitutional authority to limit free speech—"Congress shall make no law . . . abridging the freedom of speech"—but whether spending money is *equivalent* to speech is a point of contention among many. Imagine that the court had upheld expenditure limits on campaigns. One could argue that this would not have limited a campaign's speech, under the presumption that campaign rallies, door-knocking, and volunteer efforts do not require much money. Indeed, most campaigns staff their headquarters with volunteers. No expenditure limit could stop a candidate from coordinating volunteers to devote their energies to the election or from talking with voters.

Still, such an argument is a hard sell to many, in part because money is connected to so much of what candidates do in an election. In *Buckley*, the court held that direct limits on campaign expenditures had a major effect on how much speech voters would hear from those running for office. The contribution limits, however, were easier to justify and defend. Because contributions to candidates could plausibly create a relationship between donor and candidate that might raise concerns of bribery and corruption, limits on direct contributions to candidates were deemed valid.

Buckley allows expenditure limits only in voluntary public funding systems. This is most important for presidential elections. Congress established in the late 1960s and again in the early 1970s a system of public funding for presidential elections, by which candidates receive a lump sum for the general election in exchange for limiting their campaign spending to the amount of that grant.[6] The court reasoned that because the system was voluntary, candidates who opted into the system were consenting to limit their speech. Notably, every major presidential candidate between 1976 and 2004 opted into the general election system. After Watergate, presidential candidates wanted to create the impression that moneyed interests were not running the show.[7] But in 2008 Barack Obama opted out, and in 2012 both Obama and Republican nominee Mitt Romney opted out. Because candidates can raise money today online (which has facilitated fund-raising efforts) and given the considerable expense of running a presidential campaign, it is now almost unthinkable that any major party candidate for president in a future election would voluntarily limit his or her spending in primary and general election campaigns.

There is one campaign finance provision that often goes unnoticed by many observers of politics but that is especially important when it comes to buying political advertising. The 1971 FECA established that for a certain window before Election Day, broadcasters must sell advertising space to candidates at the **lowest unit rate**. This essentially means that candidates must be charged the least expensive rate that is normally offered by the broadcaster for the requested airtime.[8] This is an incredibly important provision that helps candidates manage, to some extent, the cost of their campaign advertising. To be sure, it is not always clear what the lowest rate is because the cost of advertising varies across markets and time of day and is determined by individual television stations, and preemptible and non-preemptible ad space have different rates. Still, giving candidates some modest discount on political advertising helps moderate the overall cost of elections—at least to some extent.

Traditional Party Committees

The campaign finance reforms and judicial decisions of the 1970s put political parties at an immediate disadvantage in the electoral arena. The new rules restricted how much parties could contribute to candidates' campaigns and capped what they could spend in coordination with candidates. This coordination cap was set at ten thousand dollars for House candidates and varied for Senate candidates depending on the state's voting-age population. All limits were indexed to inflation, so in 2014, the parties could engage in coordinated spending up to $47,200 with a House candidate and up to $349,000 with a Senate candidate from South Carolina (a state with a median population in 2010). Such sums might seem substantial until one considers that the average winning House candidate in 2012 spent $1.6 million and the average winning Senate candidate spent $10.3 million.[9]

From the parties' point of view, the most damaging element of the reforms of the 1970s was a ban on **independent expenditures** by parties—that is, additional spending aimed at helping a candidate that is not coordinated with the candidate's campaign. This ban was affirmed for parties in *Buckley* even though the court struck down spending limits for candidates, groups, and individuals. Along with the contribution and coordination caps, this significantly handicapped parties. During the two decades following the reforms of the 1970s, parties played second fiddle to candidates in federal elections, and scholars have noted the diminished role of parties in the electorate during that period (and an associated growth in self-identified independent voters)[10] as well as a decline in their role in determining presidential nominees.[11]

A sea change began in the 1990s, though. In 1996, the Supreme Court in *Colorado Republican Federal Campaign Committee et al. v. Federal Election Commission* freed the parties to make unlimited independent expenditures on behalf of candidates. The court ruled that the prohibition of such expenditures was an infringement on the parties' First Amendment rights. The court's reasoning was that, because the expenditures were made without the candidate's knowledge, they should not be considered direct contributions to candidates' campaigns. This rationale made the treatment of party spending consistent with the court's treatment of PAC and individual spending in *Buckley*.

A more significant development in the 1990s was that the parties started to exploit a loophole in campaign finance laws that allowed them to raise and spend **soft money** to help federal candidates. Soft money is raised outside the regulated system of federal campaign finance laws from otherwise prohibited sources, such as corporations and unions. **Hard money**, in contrast, is collected within the limits prescribed by campaign finance laws and used directly for federal elections. Why were parties able to collect soft money? Such funds had been legal for parties to use since the 1980s, after they argued to the FEC that not all their expenditures were related to federal campaigns; some were intended to help state and local candidates and to more generally promote the party's image. Imagine a Republican Party ad or brochure touting small government and personal responsibility: the party argued that such efforts were outside the intended scope of campaign finance laws.

The soft money allowance was not much of an issue in the 1980s, when parties tended to use soft money for these party-building purposes. But during the mid-1990s, the federal courts ruled that interest groups, and by extension parties, could use unregulated funds to pay for ads that both promoted issues and featured federal candidates.[12] If an ad from an interest group or party included a set of particular words or phrases, then the ad was considered **express advocacy** and thus subject to stringent funding guidelines. These **magic words**, first listed in a footnote of the *Buckley* decision, were: "vote for," "elect," "support," "cast your ballot for," "Smith for Congress," "vote against," "defeat," and "reject." But absent them, the ad was considered issue education or **issue advocacy**, and thus could be paid for with soft money. Suddenly parties saw an opening to pay for ads and brochures that touted their core values but that also featured a candidate and promoted his or her virtues (or that warned more broadly of the vices of the opposing party).

Imagine a Democratic Party ad that tells voters about a whole host of legislative accomplishments by an incumbent senator or president. The ad then finishes by urging voters to "Vote for [the candidate] in November." This ad is clearly election-related, as evidenced by the magic phrase "vote for," and consequently it must be funded by the party's hard money account. Now imagine the same ad but with an ending that urges viewers to "contact [the candidate] and thank him for his efforts." Both ads, in this example, air on the same day at the same time in the same media market, but on separate stations. The absence of the "vote for" tagline in the second ad, however, means it is a soft money ad that can be funded with huge corporate or union checks.

Parties increased their soft money outlays significantly in the 1990s. For example, the parties' congressional campaign committees (such as the Democratic Congressional Campaign Committee and the Republican National Senatorial Committee) increased their soft money spending from eighty million dollars in 1996 to just under three hundred million dollars in 2002. The impetus for these increased electoral efforts was not just the court cases that seemed to permit them. It was also the growing polarization between Democrats and Republicans and the razor-thin margins that determined control of Congress, not to mention the contentious and tight 2000 presidential election. Parties needed every dollar they could find to fight for control in Washington, DC.[13]

Consequently, the parties became incredibly adept at convincing interest groups and individuals to give soft money donations. A majority of soft money came from interest groups, including corporations and unions; in fact, corporate donations account for about 40 percent of all soft money that parties raised between 1992 and 2002.[14] Thus, by exploiting soft money as an avenue for influence, party organizations went from being marginalized as political actors in the 1970s and 1980s to being a focal point of federal campaigns.[15]

This is clear when we look at party advertising in the 2000 election cycle, a year during which control of the House and Senate were up for grabs and the presidential race was tight. Parties sponsored 65 percent of all the general election television ads in the presidential race and about one in every four House and Senate ads. The number for the presidential race is particularly high because both Gore and Bush were limited (voluntarily) to the public funding grant. This capped each campaign's spending at $67.5 million, and both candidates looked to the parties' soft money accounts for a significant boost and competitive advantage.

The prevalence of soft money in this period motivated Congress to majorly overhaul campaign finance law in 2002. The **Bipartisan Campaign Reform Act (BCRA)** outlawed the parties' use of soft money and forced the parties to use only regulated hard money for any and all expenditures. Because soft money was relatively easy to raise—it could come in any increment and often arrived in million-dollar checks—the ban on soft money was expected to weaken the influence of political parties.[16]

In some ways, however, the law merely moved the parties' fund-raising into the world of hard money. They were forced to become more aggressive in courting small-donor checks, and they proved up to the task. See, for example, the totals reported in Table 2.1, which shows the contributions received by the major party committees in the six elections before and after the passage of BCRA. In the 2004 presidential cycle, parties increased their hard money totals by 129 percent over the 2000 election. In 2006, they boosted their hard money haul by about 82 percent over the previous midterm election in 2002. The transition to hard money–only donations was not easy, but the parties proved remarkably resilient in the face of attempts to undermine their organizational and electoral influence. These fund-raising changes also corresponded to new initiatives in both parties to build stronger state-level parties. Most notably, the Democratic Party's fifty-state strategy, implemented by party chair Howard Dean in 2005 and 2006 to make the party strong nationwide, was paid for with hard money.[17]

All told, the parties have become powerful organizations capable of influencing federal elections in ways unforeseen by reformers of the 1970s. Recent developments appear to have shifted additional powers back to parties. The Supreme Court in *McCutcheon v. Federal Election Commission* (2014) overturned one of the more arcane provisions of FECA, that an individual donor's hard money contribution had to fall under the maximum allowed when totaled across all candidates and parties. The court overturned this provision, arguing that it served no compelling governmental interest, which meant that donors could give the hard money maximum to as many candidates as were running. This was expected to help party committees, which could facilitate

Table 2.1: Contribution Totals from Individuals to Party Committees (Hard Money)

	Total	Relative change from before BCRA
1992	$245,521,103	
1994	216,848,652	
1996	394,680,901	
1998	253,161,236	
2000	445,699,207	
2002	373,720,097	
2004	1,022,461,043	129.41%
2006	679,073,420	81.71%
2008	761,154,753	
2010	685,460,803	
2012	713,178,202	
2014	746,309,133	

Totals include DNC, RNC, and both parties' House and Senate campaigns. BCRA first applied to the 2004 election; spending for the 2004 and 2006 elections are compared to, respectively, the previous presidential and midterm election. Totals are not adjusted for inflation. *Source*: Federal Election Commission

that giving. In late 2014, parties got an additional boost when, as part of its bill to keep the government open, Congress passed minor adjustments to campaign finance laws that raised the hard money limits on parties for individual donors. Those additional funds could not be used for electoral purposes, but they still increased the hard money totals that parties could accumulate.

Interest Groups

Interest groups have always been a bigger concern than parties for advocates of campaign finance reform. Indeed, a comprehensive review of the history of campaign finance reform reveals that corporations (and their wealthy executives) and unions were the focus of most major campaign finance reform efforts in the twentieth century. Laws passed in 1907 (banning corporate contributions) and 1947 (banning union contributions) were explicitly focused on interest groups.

Interest-group electioneering after FECA and *Buckley,* which overturned FECA's limits on independent expenditures by interest groups but preserved the ban on candidate and party contributions by corporations and unions, can be grouped into three phases. In the first phase, between 1976 and the mid-1990s, most interest groups, if they were interested in electoral politics, formed PACs and contributed modest sums to candidates. Some groups aired ads that advocated for or against federal candidates, but such efforts paled in comparison to the electioneering done by candidates.[18]

Things started to change in the mid-1990s, the second phase. The polarization between Democrats and Republicans then motivated many interest groups to invest more in elections. While PACs can spend unlimited amounts to air ads, those funds are subject to strict donor contribution limits. As such, the soft money loopholes that parties exploited were similarly exploited by many interest groups, allowing them to more easily raise large sums of money. By avoiding "magic words," groups produced ads that were considered issue advocacy and therefore protected speech that posed, in the eyes of the federal courts, no real threat of corruption.

Congress tried to clamp down on these developments in much the same way that it did with its ban on the parties' use of soft money. BCRA mandated that radio and television ads from interest groups that mentioned or pictured federal candidates and aired close to elections had to be paid for through PAC accounts. But the limits of these new rules were immediately tested by outside groups, who continued to devise ways around the new reforms. For example, the BCRA provisions outlined above seemed to apply directly to groups funded by corporations and unions. But what about issue advocacy groups, often referred to as "527s" in reference to the applicable section of the tax code, that were funded solely by individual contributions, albeit large ones? This question gained prominence in 2004 when one such group, the Swift Boat Veterans for Truth, aggressively attacked the Democratic presidential nominee, John Kerry. Swift Boat Veterans claimed that it wasn't a PAC and therefore was not subject to the new BCRA rules.

The search for loopholes ended—and the third phase began—when the BCRA reforms in this area were finally overturned in one of the most significant Supreme Court cases in recent memory. In *Citizens United v Federal Election Commission* (2010), five of the nine justices argued that restrictions on interest-group electioneering, including the ban on corporations and unions using general treasury funds for ads that used the magic words, were unconstitutional under the First Amendment. The case concerned the definition of a political ad. Citizens United, an interest group funded in part by corporate donors, wanted to pay to have a critical documentary they made about Hillary Clinton distributed as video-on-demand on cable television for free. The question of the case could have been very narrowly defined as whether documentary-length videos constitute political ads (to which the justices could have said no, resolving the case without much fanfare), but the justices expanded the scope of the case to overturn all restrictions on interest-group electioneering. What remained were limits on direct contributions to candidates and parties.

Thus, in order to comply with the court's ruling in *Citizens United*, the Federal Election Commission permitted the creation of the super PAC, a new type of group that could explicitly advocate for and against candidates and could raise unlimited funds but could not contribute to a candidate's campaign. Given their flexibility, super PACs proved very popular, but there was one small drawback: the FEC required that they report their donors. But what if you are a billionaire who wants to help a candidate to the tune of a few million dollars, but you don't want journalists or the public to know? In that case, you give money to a group organized as a nonprofit: a 501c group. Such groups, also known as **dark money** groups, are allowed to collect unlimited amounts and to avoid all public disclosure of their donors. 501c groups were not invented for campaign financing purposes—they have long existed as tax classifications (for example, c4s are social welfare groups, c5s are labor unions, c6s are business groups)—but they have proved incredibly important to outside groups looking for a way to influence elections without having to itemize donations with the FEC. The only catch is that their political activities cannot be their primary purpose.

The rise of dark money groups has spawned much debate about whether additional rules concerning the disclosure of donors are necessary. Disclosure has long been seen as a public good in campaign finance. Indeed, some of the earliest campaign finance laws in the twentieth century were focused on disclosure. The 1910 Publicity Act and the 1925 Federal Corrupt Practices Act, in particular, mandated that candidates report their contributions and expenditures to the federal government. The fact that wealthy individuals, corporations, and unions can now spend millions of dollars to influence a race by funneling it through a dark money group—without the public knowing the source of that money—is troubling to many observers.

In sum, the *Citizens United* decision significantly empowered interest groups, allowing them to raise and spend unlimited amounts. The decision did not create dark money groups, but it did make channeling money through such groups, as a way to hide the names of donors, much more attractive. This development is considered by many to be as troubling as any other recent change in campaign finance and is one we will examine in more depth later in this chapter.

THE IMPACT OF THE RULES

The rules of campaign finance have many implications for the study of political advertising. For example, changes in the rules have resulted in changes in *who* is sponsoring the bulk of political advertising. During the period of party soft money, party-sponsored ad spending exceeded spending by outside groups. Since *Citizens United*, super PAC and 501c spending have surpassed party spending. We will document more completely these types of changes in ad sponsorship in Chapter 3.

There are many other trends in ad spending that can be tied directly to the rules of campaign finance. In the remainder of this chapter, we highlight three. The first centers on federal candidates and the amount of money they devote to airing ads. Much of the discussion of campaign finance focuses on parties and interest groups—and rightly so, given that most changes in the last generation have been about those political actors. But candidates are embedded in a campaign finance environment in which there are tight restrictions on how they can raise money. How much of what candidates raise goes to fund television, radio, and Internet advertising? The second and third trends discussed in this section focus on the spending of parties and groups. How much do sponsors pay to air their messages, and how do changes in ad sponsorship affect the cost of campaigns? What kinds of interest groups sponsor ads, and what concerns have been raised about transparency and tracking the sources of campaign dollars?

Trend 1: The Cost of Media for Candidates

One goal of campaign finance reform in the early 1970s was to limit how much candidates could spend on television advertising. As noted earlier, one very specific provision of the 1971 campaign finance reform law limited the percentage of a candidate's budget that could be spent on media. That law was overturned by the justices in *Buckley*, which has ended up forcing candidates into ads arms races. Consequently, today's candidates often complain about the challenge of raising enough money to air ads. It is not uncommon to hear stories of members of Congress leaving their congressional offices, walking across the street to party headquarters (since they are prohibited from using their government offices and phones for fund-raising), and spending six to eight hours "dialing for dollars," begging potential donors for campaign contributions. This is partly why the rules of campaign finance are so important for campaign advertising.[19]

How much do candidates actually spend on ads and media, though? This is not easy to get a handle on. Candidates send quarterly itemized reports on spending to the Federal Election Commission, but there is no standard way to categorize expenditures. For example, one candidate might report ad spending as "media" while another might classify it as "persuasion efforts." Another might simply label it "campaigning." Gary Jacobson, in his authoritative book on congressional elections, asserts that, based on a study of FEC-reported disbursements in the early 1990s, mass media advertising "absorbs about 45 percent of a typical campaign budget."[20] However, he does not specify whether that refers to all congressional races or just competitive ones. A report from media consultants Borrell Associates in early 2012 projects that $9.8 billion would be spent on all forms of media in local, state, and federal elections that year, and 57 percent of that total—$5.6 billion—would be spent on broadcast television specifically.[21]

Two sources of data for Senate candidates' expenditures in 2012 and 2014 are useful for quantifying the percentage of money spent on media and advertising. The first, from the Wesleyan Media Project (WMP), is the estimated money spent on buying local broadcast ads in each election year. The totals in this database refer only to the estimated cost of buying ads on local television stations; they exclude ad costs for local cable, radio, print, and the Internet, as well as the costs of producing the ad and hiring consultants to provide advice on how to make and distribute the ad. The second source of data is the itemized FEC disbursement reports for congressional candidates. Here, we had to apply some care in categorizing expenditures before analyzing the data.[22] We didn't include the reported cost of direct mail, printing costs, or postage in the media costs we examined. Instead, we looked at the cost of ads on broadcast and digital cable, radio, the Internet, and billboards, as well as reported production costs, media consulting costs, and expenditures labeled more broadly as "media." Choosing to include any expenditure that the candidate indicated as advertising- or media-related allowed us to see more clearly how much money a candidate commits to the task of designing, producing, filming, and airing messages to the voting public.

Figure 2.1 shows media costs as a percentage of Senate candidate budgets in 2012 and 2014. The average across all major party candidates was 43 percent. Some candidates reported lower expenditures than that, but many far exceeded it. For example, Republican Senate candidate Josh Mandel of Ohio reported spending nearly $19 million total in 2012; the FEC data show that over $12 million of that was media expenditures, about two-thirds of his total reported spending.

**Figure 2.1: Media Spending by Candidates as Percentage of Total
Budget**

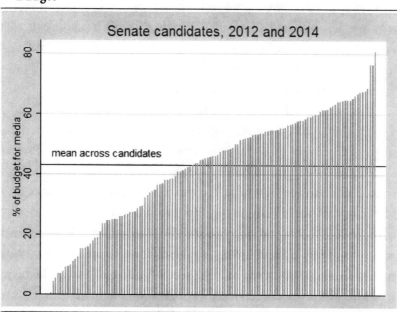

Each bar represents a particular candidate. *Source:* Raw data from the Federal Election
Commission

The WMP data estimate that his campaign spent just over $7 million
to buy ads on local broadcast television stations, which is 38 percent
of his total campaign spending. Indeed, based on the WMP estimates,
Senate candidates on average spent 32 percent of their total campaign
budgets just to buy space on local broadcast television.

Advertising and media spending by the Obama and Romney campaigns in 2012 provides a nice point of comparison for the Senate figures. Obama reported spending $683 million total in 2012, and Romney
reported spending $433 million. According to the WMP data, Obama
spent $310 million on local broadcast or national cable television ad-
vertising, which was 45 percent of his total spending. The Center for
Responsive Politics (CRP) calculated that Obama spent $483 million
in total media-related costs, or 71 percent of his reported expenditures.

The WMP data show Romney spent $141 million on local broadcast ads (excluding expenditures totaling $24 million that were shared with the Republican National Committee), which amounted to 33 percent of his total campaign spending. Romney spent $240 million in media-related costs, according to the CRP, which is 55 percent of his campaign's total spending.

That the Obama campaign committed just over 70 percent of its sizable budget to media and television airtime speaks to its importance in presidential elections. But advertising is an important share of total campaign expenditures even in lower-profile House races. House candidates are harder to compare in this regard because some districts are in dense urban markets where television advertising is not efficient because it reaches many voters who live outside the district. Still, if we restrict the analysis to the nearly 750 candidates in 2012 and 2014 who itemized at least one million dollars in expenditures, the average House campaign reported spending 33 percent of its total campaign budget on media-related activities.

Ultimately, then, media—and televised political advertising specifically—makes up a sizeable chunk of a campaign's budget. This is unlikely to change at any point in the near future. Advertising is especially important in the United States because politicians represent so many people. The average House district now has over seven hundred thousand people,[23] which is way too many for any one candidate to meet face to face. And of course, senators, governors, and presidents represent many more than seven hundred thousand people. On top of this, because there are no requirements that broadcasters give candidates or parties free airtime, something that exists in many countries, campaigns must rely on paid advertising.

Trend 2: The Cost of an Ad for Parties and Interest Groups

Candidates' ad spending tells only part of the story. It's true that they spend a lot of money on campaign ads, but candidates also benefit from the lowest unit rate. Party and interest groups do not similarly benefit from this rule, so when there is substantial competition for airtime, they pay hefty sums—as much as the market will bear. Indeed, the market for airtime in some of the most competitive House and Senate races is a major boon to the bottom lines of broadcast television stations.

How much sponsors pay for advertising is sometimes difficult to determine, even in the age of "big data." One possible source of information is local broadcast stations, which are required by law to keep a file available to the public that contains contracts between political ad sponsors and the station. Before 2012 these files were largely stored as hard copies at the television stations. Citizens, scholars, and political opponents could only search the files by hand, station by station, hard copy by hard copy. Assembling a comprehensive database of ad costs across stations and markets was nearly impossible.

In 2012, the **Federal Communications Commission (FCC)**, the government agency that regulates broadcast media, including television and radio, mandated that broadcast stations in the fifty largest media markets upload their public files to the FCC website. In 2014, the FCC expanded the rule to cover all stations in the nation's 210 media markets. These mandates are a major advance for scholarship, but there still is a significant challenge in standardizing the data. Stations need only upload the scanned versions of the contracts, and there is no uniform data-reporting standard. Still, the 2014 data on the FCC website (posted online for ad contracts beginning on or after July 1) represent the universe of data on broadcast ad costs.

Another source of spending information is the WMP data, which was used in the previous section to calculate ad costs for candidates, and similar data from the Wisconsin Advertising Project (a predecessor to the WMP). These data are informed by a rigorous attempt to capture the likely cost of political ads in media markets of different sizes and population density. But they may not reflect the actual amounts paid by ad sponsors, especially when parties and interest groups end up in bidding wars over premium ad space. Only the ad buy contracts, which list the agreed-on price, can show the true costs. Thus, we still faced the challenge of collecting and standardizing the

FCC data. To address this, we partnered with Patrick Ruffini, who runs Echelon Insights, a political research and intelligence firm. His company devoted considerable efforts to collecting each contract from the FCC and entering its data into a spreadsheet, taking care to include amended or changed terms. The resulting set of data allows us to document the price-per-spot differences among sponsors in competitive markets.

The raw data are extensive. For example, they include all sponsors of ads in local, state, and federal races, each week they advertised, and each television station on which they bought ad space. Figure 2.2 shows the median price per spot across all markets in the twenty weeks before the election for each type of sponsor—candidates, parties, and interest groups.[24] For candidates in House and Senate races, the median cost per ad is about two hundred dollars between July 1 and Election Day, with just slight increases as the campaign comes to a close. Of course, these data hide considerable diversity in ad costs introduced by variations in market size, the size of the audience for a particular program, and the desirability of a program's audience for advertisers. Ad costs can also depend on whether candidates reserve ad spots in advance—a sort of Sam's Club approach that offers discounts for buying in bulk—or buy ads week to week. Still, the relative stability of prices (as demonstrated in the graph) thanks to the "lowest unit rate" rule is important for candidates. Knowing ad prices are unlikely to spike astronomically for them in the final days helps them better establish fund-raising goals throughout the campaign, plan for the rough costs of advertising at the end of a campaign, and commit to a last-minute deluge of ads if needed in a tight race.

There is far less predictability for groups and party committees. For these sponsors, ad costs spike as Election Day draws near. In House races, the median cost across markets more than triples for party committees and interest groups; it doubles for these same sponsors in Senate races. One reason for such dramatic changes is the absence of the "lowest unit rate" rule for outside groups and party committees. A super PAC advocating for a candidate close to the election faces the

Figure 2.2: Ad Costs by Sponsor and Week in House and Senate Races

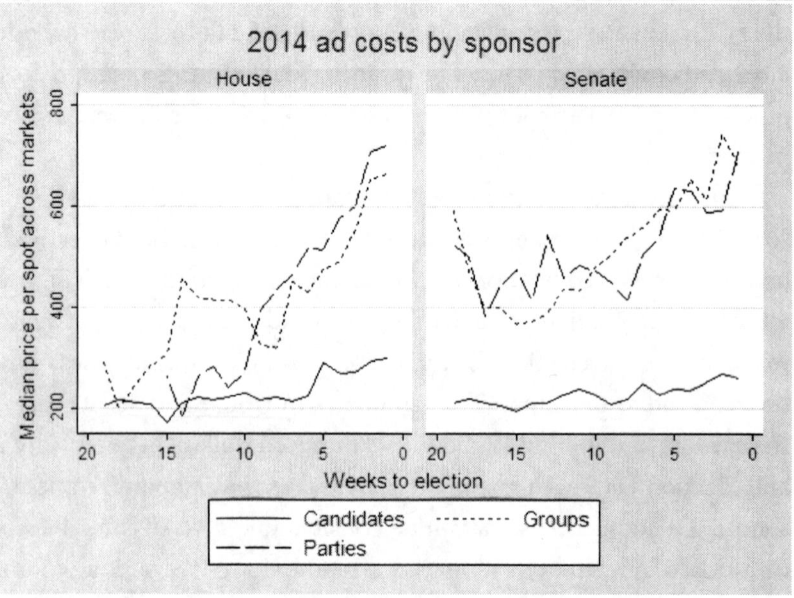

2014 ad costs by sponsor

Source: Patrick Ruffini, Echelon Insights

daunting challenge of paying for airtime that is heavily desired by competing groups and party committees. If there are a number of advertisers that want ad space during the local news the night before the election, broadcast stations are in the driver's seat. They can demand whatever they think super PACs and party committees can afford to pay. Thus, the presence of outside money in federal elections has had the effect of increasing the overall cost of campaigns. Outside groups pay more for ads, and to the extent that the entrepreneurs in those groups are seeking a significant stake in the conduct and content of political campaigns, they are "overpaying"—certainly compared to their candidate allies.

The skyrocketing of ad prices post–*Citizens United* could change ad-buying strategies in elections to come. As competition for airtime increases and the gap between what candidates pay for ads and what groups pay rises even more, donors may begin to direct more of their dollars to candidates. Another possibility is that it may lead to a division of labor in which groups advertise more prior to the "lowest unit rate" window and then move their resources to online or direct-contact activities (for example, "get out the vote" efforts) as Election Day nears. Thus, the "lowest unit rate" provision may help to mitigate recent changes in campaign finance law that have benefitted groups.

Trend 3: Dark Money and Disclosure

One final trend concerns the transparency surrounding sponsors of political ads. Candidates and party committees are completely transparent in that they submit regular reports to the Federal Election Commission detailing their contributions and expenditures. Most interest groups that are involved in elections also submit reports to the FEC, but these reports are often less comprehensive.

PACs that make contributions directly to candidates report the source of their funds and the contributions they make to candidates to the FEC, so transparency is less of a concern for these groups. But two types of groups that produce uncoordinated political ads advocating for issue positions and/or attacking candidates have more gaps in disclosure. The first type is super PACs, which actually must report contributions and expenditures but can accept contributions of unlimited size from groups that are not fully transparent. The second type is 501c nonprofits. Most of the 501c organizations active in politics are organized as 501c4s. Their principal goal is to advance social welfare, but they are permitted to do some electioneering so long as it is not their primary purpose. This "primary purpose" standard—and the question of what constitutes electioneering—has created an opportunity for these types of organizations to invest in electoral politics with candidate ads. A 501c4 organization does not need to publicly disclose donors.

How much interest-group advertising is funded by organizations that disclose their donors? To find out, let's look at groups that sponsored ads in the congressional elections in 2012 and 2014 and in the presidential election of 2012. Each group can be categorized into one of three types: (1) fully transparent groups, such as super PACs; (2) dark money groups that do not disclose any donors; and (3) partial-disclosure groups. The last category consists of groups that take on multiple legal forms—one group could be both a super PAC and a 501c4—and groups that voluntarily disclose some of their donors even if they are not required to do so by law.

Figure 2.3 shows the degree of disclosure by the race type and party (full and partial disclosure groups are combined here). Two points stand out. First, dark money ads, defined here as those that do not disclose any donors, are not the majority of interest-group-sponsored ads. A great percentage of the ads aired on behalf of Democratic candidates in 2012 and 2014 were sponsored by groups who report some or all of their contributions to the Federal Election Commission. Second, pro-Republican groups were more dependent on dark money than were Democrats in both 2012 and 2014. In recent years, Democrats have tended to rely on super PACs such as Priorities USA (pro-Obama), House Majority PAC, and Majority PAC. These super PACs have operated essentially as soft money extensions of the party committees. Republicans, in contrast, have relied more heavily on 501c4 organizations, such as Crossroads GPS and the US Chamber of Commerce, and tea party groups such as American Action Network.

That the source of most ad money is disclosed does not imply that concerns about lack of disclosure are misplaced. In fact, dark money may grow in future elections, and even fully transparent super PACs accept huge checks from sources that are not as transparent. Perhaps the best example of this is the case of comedian Stephen Colbert's super PAC, Americans for a Better Tomorrow, Tomorrow, which he established with the help of election lawyer Trevor Potter. Colbert discussed this on his show, *The Colbert Report,* as part of a comic skit to demonstrate one effect of the *Citizens United* decision. To show how super PACs are not as transparent as we might like, Colbert set up a parallel 501c4, asked viewers to donate to the nonprofit, and then contributed those sums to the super PAC.

Colbert's perfectly legal actions brought home to American voters how easy it is to funnel vast sums into a campaign for office without

Figure 2.3: Advertising Disclosure by Race and Party

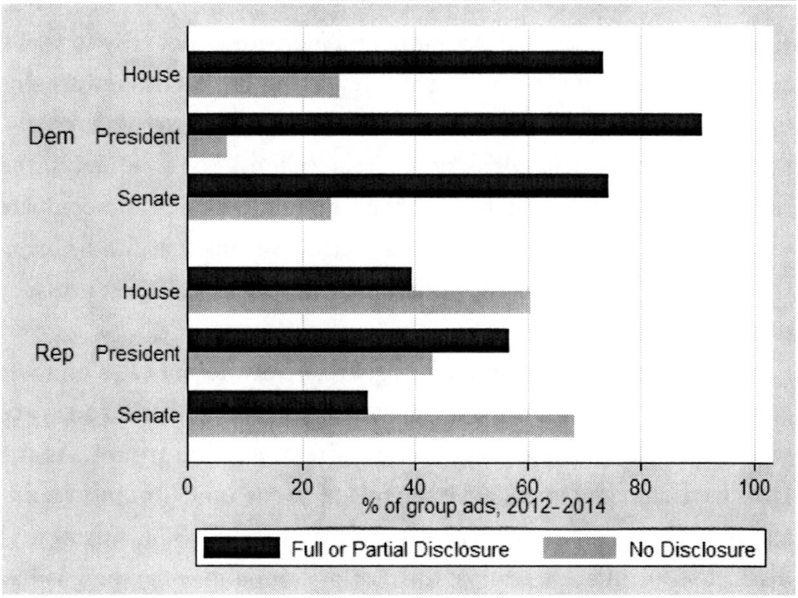

Source: Wesleyan Media Project and the Center for Responsive Politics

anyone knowing where the money came from. But why should the voting public know who is funding the campaign messages that they receive? First, when people do not know who is backing an ad, they have no basis for evaluating the ad's arguments. In deciding whether to believe a claim that a member of Congress is a champion of the environment, it helps to know whether the money that paid for the ad came from an executive at Exxon or thousands of small donors pooling their resources. Second, knowing who paid for an ad can help journalists root out corruption. It is much easier to cry foul when a member of Congress introduces a bill favorable to the oil industry if we know that an Exxon executive spent three million dollars on ads supporting that person in the previous election.

CONCLUSION

The source of money that pays for campaign ads is not easy to track, and rules governing the raising and reporting of that money are difficult to comprehend. The rules are complex—and ever-changing—because of new regulations and court decisions. For candidates, the rules have largely been stable, but the demand to air ads and compete with parties and interest groups for airtime means that fund-raising within contribution and coordination limits puts significant pressure on candidates.

On the other hand, candidates get relatively decent rates on their airtime, but this has created a vigorous market for preferred ad space among the party committees and a cadre of outside groups. As the rules have changed to enhance the role of parties and groups in political advertising, especially with fewer restrictions on fund-raising and disclosure for interest groups, the cost of competitive campaigns has risen above what it would be if candidates were the dominant political spenders.

There is nothing inherently wrong with campaigns costing a lot of money; "cheap" campaigns are perhaps not a desirable goal in a democracy. In fact, a lot of political science research demonstrates that campaigning has positive effects on what citizens know about politics and their ability to make informed vote choices. Presumably, then, more abundant interest-group advertising can contribute relevant information that voters can use in making choices between candidates. What's more important than the cost of advertising is the disclosure of where ad money originates. Voters should be able to investigate the groups who are trying to lobby them for their votes, and they should be able to weigh the messages they see with the full knowledge of who is financially backing those messages.

Because so much of what campaigns, parties, and groups raise is devoted to producing and purchasing television advertising, this chapter's discussion of the rules that govern the financing of American elections is an important antecedent to the rest of the book. In the next chapter, we take advantage of the rich data available on political advertising volume to look at important changes in ad content over time.

DISCUSSION QUESTIONS

1. What is the "lowest unit rate" provision? What are some of the consequences of this provision for candidates and groups when it comes to purchasing political advertising? How might it indirectly affect voters?
2. Why is dark money spending such a concern for advocates of campaign finance reform? What arguments could be made in favor of dark money spending?
3. Why are presidential candidates opting out of the system of public financing nowadays? What impact is that having on political advertising spending and, ultimately, on voters?
4. The content of political advertising is clearly political speech protected by the First Amendment. No congressional law could ban what candidates can say to voters. But is the money contributed to candidates—and used to purchase airtime—and the money spent by outside groups and parties also rightly understood as speech?

NOTES

1. There were reforms along the way, of course, most notably the Taft-Hartley Act in 1947, which banned unions from contributing to candidates and making pro-candidate expenditures. That was an important legislative change, but most historians of campaign finance see two comprehensive reform cycles in the twentieth century: the set of rules established with the Federal Corrupt Practices Act of 1910 and the 1971/1974 FECA reforms. See Robert Mutch, *Buying the Vote: A History of Campaign Finance Reform* (New York: Oxford University Press, 2014).

2. Candidates may also use personal funds to finance their campaigns, without limits.

3. Some PACs are unaffiliated with a sponsoring organization; these are most commonly ideological groups pushing for certain social reforms. These unconnected PACs can accept contributions from any American citizen.

4. See Mark Rozell, Clyde Wilcox, and Michael Franz, "Interest Groups and Candidates," chap. 3 in *Interest Groups in American Campaigns: The New Face of Electioneering*, 3rd ed., (New York: Oxford University Press, 2012).

5. Anthony Corrado, "Money and Politics: A History of Campaign Finance Law," in *The New Campaign Finance Sourcebook*, ed. Anthony Corrado, Thomas Mann, Daniel Ortiz, and Trevor Potter (Washington, DC: Brookings Institution Press, 2005), 21, 23.

6. There is also a public funding system for presidential nominations, in which candidates agree to limit spending in primary states in exchange for federal matching of private contributions. The FECA of 1974 established this primary and general election system, but its genesis is also in the Presidential Campaign Fund Act of 1966 and the Revenue Act of 1971.

7. There were limits to this display, however. As soft money for parties exploded, candidates like Al Gore and George Bush in 2000 could easily accept the public funding—and claim they were following campaign finance laws that limited candidate spending—while relying on the extensive party efforts organized on their behalf.

8. This provision only applies in the forty-five days before a primary election and in the sixty days before a general election.

9. Campaign Finance Institute, *Cost of Winning a Seat*, accessed January 23, 2015, http://www.cfinst.org/federal/congress.aspx.

10. Martin Wattenberg, *The Decline of American Political Parties, 1952–1994* (Cambridge, MA: Harvard University Press, 1996). See also Larry Bartels, "Partisanship and Voting Behavior, 1952–1996," *American Journal of Political Science* 44, no. 1 (1996): 35–50.

11. Nelson Polsby, *Consequences of Party Reform* (New York: Oxford University Press, 1983); Graham Wilson, *Interest Groups in the United States* (Oxford: Clarendon Press, 1981).

12. See, for example, *FEC v. Christian Action Network* (1997) and *Maine Right to Life Committee v. FEC* (1996).

13. Michael M. Franz, *Choices and Changes: Interest Groups in the Electoral Process* (Philadelphia: Temple University Press, 2007).

14. This is based on our own analysis of soft money donations between 1992 and 2002.

15. The national parties worked on increasing their organizational capacity throughout the late 1970s and 1980s. See Leon Epstein, *Political Parties in the American Mold* (Madison, WI: University of Wisconsin Press, 1986), 208–225. It

was this increased capacity that undoubtedly helped the parties take advantage of the soft money opportunity in the 1990s and early 2000s.

16. Ray La Raja, *Small Change: Money, Political Parties, and Campaign Finance Reform* (Chicago: University of Chicago Press, 2007).

17. Ari Berman, *Herding Donkeys: The Fight to Rebuild the Democratic Party and Reshape American Politics* (New York: Farrar, Straus, and Giroux, 2010).

18. Rozell, Wilcox, and Franz, *Interest Groups in American Campaigns.*

19. See Stephen Ansolabehere, Alan Gerber, and James Snyder, "Does TV Advertising Explain the Rise of Campaign Spending? A Study of Campaign Spending and Broadcast Advertising Prices in US House Elections in the 1990s and 1970s" (working paper, Harvard University, 2001). The authors argue that the cost of broadcast advertising is not the primary culprit in the rising costs of campaigns. They find evidence that in high-cost media markets, candidates often forgo advertising in favor of comparatively cheaper voter outreach, such as direct mail. Their study examines candidates in the 1970s and 1990s, and presumably their point is still relevant in an era of less-pricey digital media.

20. Gary Jacobson, *The Politics of Congressional Elections,* 8th ed. (Upper Saddle River, NJ: Pearson, 2013), 99.

21. Applying this figure to a total cost of elections up and down the ballot is quite difficult, since there is no central database that collects the costs of local and statewide elections. However, the Center for Responsive Politics reported that candidates in the 2012 presidential and congressional elections spent about $4.7 billion total. (They arrived at this figure by subtracting $1.3 billion, the amount they reported was spent by parties and outside groups, from $6 billion, which they reported was the total cost of the 2012 elections.) The Borrell report estimates candidate ad spending in 2012 would be $2.3 billion (inclusive of all media), which is 49 percent of the above total. This is not far off the figure reported by Jacobson in his book for a "typical" campaign.

22. Notably, we replicated the Center for Responsive Politics' coding of the data. They report on their webpage only the media costs of winning Senate candidates. As to what the FEC files capture, the commission offers the following expenditure-reporting guidelines: "Campaign committees are required to disclose all specific disbursements that are contributions to other federal candidates or parties or other committees as well as all loan repayments. For other spending (normal operating expenses, for example, or contributions to state or local candidates), specific disbursements must be disclosed when the amount paid to any one vendor exceeds $200 in an election cycle." See Federal Election Commission, *Campaign Guide for Congressional Candidates and Committees,* June 2014, http://www.fec.gov/pdf/candgui.pdf.

23. Kristin D. Burnett, *Congressional Apportionment,* C2010BR-08, US Department of Commerce, Economics and Statistics Administration, US Census

Bureau (November 2011), https://www.census.gov/prod/cen2010/briefs/c2010br -08.pdf.

24. For this figure, coordinated ads (paid for by a party committee and a candidate) are combined with candidate ads, since those spots also qualify for the lowest unit rate.

CHAPTER 3

The Volume and Content of Political Advertising

There are two complaints we commonly hear about political advertising, especially close to Election Day. The first is that there is too much of it. The second is that there is too much negativity. Of course, whether there is "too much" of something is a subjective determination. In this chapter, we give you the hard numbers on just how much advertising is out there, how much of it is negative, and how these figures have changed over time. Finally, we examine what circumstances are likely to result in more advertising and more negativity, such as a highly competitive race.

VOLUME OF TELEVISION ADVERTISING

It may be the age of the Internet, but one would hardly know it given trends in the volume of political advertising on television over the last decade and a half. The volume of advertising during the 2012 presidential elections did not just break records, it pulverized them. There were nearly three million airings of election-related ads in federal races in 2012, a 36.5 percent increase over 2008, when there were roughly 2.19 million airings in federal races. Figure 3.1 shows the trend in the volume of presidential ads going back to 2000. The number of ads increased dramatically between 2000 and 2004, held steady between 2004 and 2008, and then increased again dramatically between 2008 and 2012.

The dramatic increase in advertising volume can be seen clearly in Colorado, where residents of the Denver media market were subjected to 55,584 presidential ads in 2012, compared to 22,621 in 2008. That's over 463 hours of television advertising for the presidential race alone, an increase of 146 percent over 2008. If one were to try to view all of those commercials, it would take nearly three weeks of around-the-clock viewing!

This increase is not limited to presidential advertising. As you can see in Figure 3.2, the volume of congressional advertising has been climbing as well, 2014 being a notable exception. (The data in both Figures 3.1 and 3.2 are limited to the top seventy-five media markets to preserve comparability over the full time period of the dataset.) Whether 2012 represents the high-water mark for political advertising remains to be seen, but the volume of US House and Senate ad airings in 2014 in all markets (not just the top seventy-five) definitely showed signs of slowing with a total of 1,585,140 airings, up just 1.8 percent over 2010 and down slightly—1.6 percent—from 2012.

Although 2014 may not have been a record-breaking year overall, advertising is not necessarily trending down, especially in the most highly competitive races. In fact, in some places it has increased. For example, 43,502 election-related ads aired in Denver in 2010 for a variety of races, including down-ballot contests, but that pales in comparison to the 72,875 that aired in 2014. Denver's 67.5 percent increase in advertising in 2014 over the 2010 midterms also earned it the distinction of having the highest volume of ads of any market in the country, with Tampa coming in a very distant second with 56,438 ads. Denver's 2014 advertising record was driven in part by the large number of competitive races in the area and in part by the fact that two powerful positions in Colorado—governor and US senator—were up for grabs.

Competitiveness and Type of Office Drives Volume

It is an extreme example, but the Denver market nicely illustrates the two biggest drivers of the volume of ads aired: the competitiveness of

Figure 3.1: Volume of Television Advertising for the Presidential Race in the Top 75 Markets, January 1–Election Day

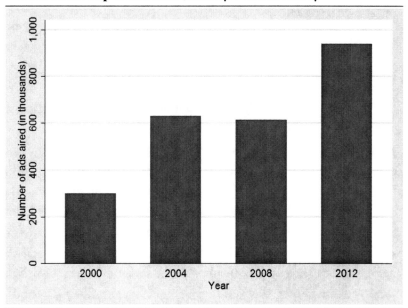

Source: Wisconsin Advertising Project and Wesleyan Media Project

Figure 3.2: Volume of Television Advertising for House and Senate Races in the Top 75 Markets, January 1–Election Day

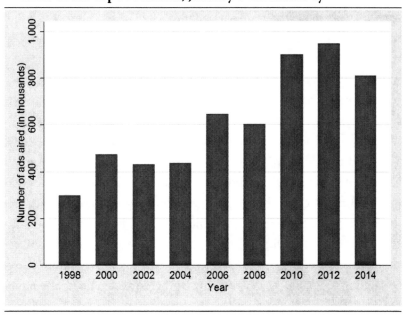

Source: Wisconsin Advertising Project and Wesleyan Media Project

the race and the type of office being contested. The fact that competitive races attract many more ads should not be surprising. Imagine you were placed in charge of an interest group's advertising budget for a fall campaign and had to choose which of three Senate races to air ads for: (1) the race in which your favored candidate is virtually guaranteed to win; (2) the race in which your favored candidate is virtually guaranteed to lose; or (3) the race that is predicted to be very close between your candidate and his or her opponent. Being a strategic actor with a (somewhat) limited budget, you may want to garner favor with the candidate you know will win, but you also know that the more people there are in higher office who support your position, the better off your organization will be. Why waste money on advertising in the races where you know it is unlikely to matter? It makes sense to target the races in which your advertising dollars may actually affect the outcome, which is exactly how advertising is allocated in the real world.

Table 3.1 displays the percentage of total ads aired for the most and least competitive races for US House and Senate in the 2012 and 2014 general-election campaigns. We relied on *Roll Call* for 2012 and the *Rothenberg Political Report* for 2014 **competitiveness ratings,** assessments of how close each House and Senate race is likely to be. As shown in the table, the bulk of congressional races in both years were for safe seats that strongly favored one party (81 percent in 2012 and nearly 86 percent in 2014). By contrast, fewer than one in ten (9 percent in 2012 and not quite 6 percent in 2014) were rated as highly competitive or toss-up races. Yet the 9 Senate and 33 House toss-ups drew the majority of advertising in 2012 (56.4 percent). Similarly, although only 5.8 percent of federal races were competitive in 2014 (7 of the 34 Senate seats and 20 of the 435 House races), over 47 percent of all federal ads that aired in 2014 were for those toss-up races.

As should be clear both from our hypothetical interest-group scenario above and the evidence presented in Table 3.1, the more competitive a particular race is perceived to be, the more advertising it is likely to attract. We will discuss advertising's effectiveness in more detail in later chapters, but it is worth noting here that theories of persuasion[1] and advertising research both suggest that when one candidate

Table 3.1: US House and Senate General Election Advertising Share by Competitiveness, September 1–Election Day

	2012		2014	
	% of races	*% of ads*	*% of races*	*% of ads*
Competitive	9.0	56.4	5.8	47.3
Lean	4.7	18.8	3.8	23.9
Favorable	5.3	11.4	4.5	15.3
Solid	81.0	13.3	85.9	13.5

Sources: Roll Call, The Rothenberg Political Report, and Wesleyan Media Project

airs more ads than another, it is likely to (but does not always) lead to increases in poll numbers for that candidate.[2] It is no wonder then that campaigns pay so much attention to what their opponents are doing on the air and attempt to at least counter, if not eliminate, any advantage in ads aired. It is easy to see how air wars can escalate in competitive races.

The other big driver of advertising volume is the type of office being contested. The biggest air wars take place in top-of-ticket races (for example, presidential, gubernatorial, and senatorial contests), for good reason: more power is at stake in races higher on the ballot on Election Day. It matters more who wins a Senate seat than a seat in the Oklahoma state legislature, and thus donors tend to direct their money to the former. In addition, higher-level offices are typically voted on by more people, and candidates need to advertise in more places to reach potential voters. At the extreme, of course, presidential candidates battle on the airwaves in multiple states, whereas gubernatorial and senatorial candidates only need to focus on media markets in their own states. Congressional candidates can typically reach most of their constituents with ads in just one or two media markets.

To put the relative scale of the different air wars in perspective, consider the following. The average number of ads aired for a Senate race between September 1 and Election Day in 2012 was just shy of

17,000, while the average number of ads aired for a House race was only 1,241 (see Table 3.2). The 2012 and 2014 elections also demonstrated that the more competitive the race, the more advertising there is. In 2012, competitive Senate contests drew an average of 37,323 ads and, in 2014, an average of 40,554 ads. The ads in the top Senate contests— Montana in 2012 (71,966 ads) and North Carolina in 2014 (69,760)— were even more abundant. While the most competitive House contests averaged roughly 9,000 ads in 2012 and 2014, which is fewer than the overall average volume of Senate advertising, toss-up House races did receive more ads than uncompetitive Senate contests. In other words, campaigns for higher offices typically produce more advertising, but competition may drastically increase the number of ads aired in any given race.

Growth in Unique Ads and Changes in Ad Sponsorship

In the past two decades there has been a modest growth in the number of unique ads, sometimes referred to as "spots" or "**creatives**," produced. A creative is distinct from an **airing**: the former refers to the unique ad itself whereas the latter refers to a particular time that creative was shown on television. The Obama campaign aired 105 different creatives between June 1 and Election Day during the 2008 general election and 120 creatives between June 1 and Election Day during the 2012 election, an increase of just over 14 percent.[3] The Romney campaign produced many more creatives (72 in total) than McCain did in 2008 (49 in total), in part because of McCain's heavy reliance on ads fully or partially sponsored by the Republican Party. As technology makes ad production and testing easier, campaigns have become increasingly adept at producing new ads to respond to changes in the news cycle or in response to an opponent's attacks.

As we noted extensively in Chapter 2, campaign finance rules matter and have a profound effect on trends in sponsorship. There are four main types of advertising sponsorship: (1) **candidate-sponsored advertising**, which is paid for by a candidate's campaign for office; (2) **party-sponsored advertising**, which is paid for by a party on behalf of a candidate; (3) **coordinated advertising**, which is aired jointly

**Table 3.2: Average Number of Ads in Congressional Races,
September 1–Election Day**

		2012	2014
SENATE	Overall average	16,991	16,402
	Competitive average	37,323	40,554
	Uncompetitive average	2,867	2,744
HOUSE	Overall average	1,241	1,011
	Competitive average	8,647	9,401
	Uncompetitive average	283	221

Sources: Roll Call, The Rothenberg Political Report, and Wesleyan Media Project

by a party and its candidate; and (4) **interest-group advertising**, which is aired by an outside group for its preferred candidate without coordinating with the candidate. In 2012, there was even **private-citizen advertising**, which, as its name suggests, is paid for by private citizens. This type of advertising is extremely rare.

Interest-group advertising has grown in recent elections thanks to shifts in the campaign finance landscape from a series of court decisions that we documented in the previous chapter, including the landmark 2010 *Citizens United* decision. As you can see in Figure 3.3, while the percentage of interest-group ads in House races in 2014 was slightly under the percentage in 2000, just prior to BCRA, it remained over 15 percent of all ads aired. On the Senate side, there has been a relatively steady increase in group activity since 2008, with 2014's 36 percent marking an all-time high over the past decade and a half.

Although interest-group advertising has grown as a share of total advertising, especially in presidential and senatorial races, candidates were still responsible for the majority of spots on the air in 2014 (see Table 3.3). More specifically, looking at the general-election period (September 1 to Election Day), 54 percent of Senate advertising was sponsored by candidates, compared to 28 percent backed by interest groups and 18 percent funded by political parties or coordinated between candidates and political parties. Party-sponsored (and party-coordinated) advertising was slightly higher in House races (31

Figure 3.3: Percentage of Party- and Interest Group-Sponsored Advertising in House and Senate Races, January 1–Election Day of Each Year

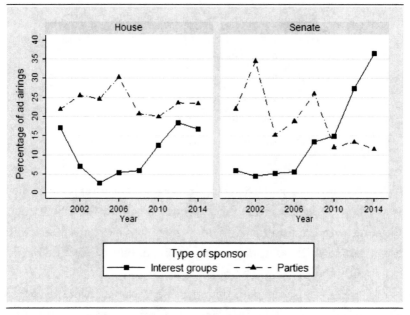

Sources: Wisconsin Advertising Project and Wesleyan Media Project

percent), but it still paled in comparison to the 56 percent of ads sponsored by the candidates themselves.

As suggested by our hypothetical interest-group scenario above, however, the balance of ads sponsored by different entities should change based on the competitiveness of the races. And indeed, as shown in Table 3.4, that is exactly what we saw in 2014. While candidates sponsored nearly all the ads aired in uncompetitive races, interest-group and party involvement increased greatly in competitive races. On the Senate side, candidates on average still sponsored the plurality of ads aired in competitive races (40 percent), but interest groups accounted for over a third (nearly 35 percent) of ads on the air while party-sponsored airings accounted for 25 percent. There were also a few races in which groups aired more ads than candidates.

Table 3.3: Percentage of 2014 Advertising Volume by Race and Sponsor, September 1–Election Day

Sponsor	Senate	House
Candidate	53.5%	55.9%
Party/coordinated	18.2%	31.4%
Interest group	28.3%	12.6%

Source: Wesleyan Media Project

Table 3.4: Percentage of 2014 Advertising Volume by Race, Sponsor, and Competitiveness, September 1–Election Day

	Sponsor	Competitive	Uncompetitive
SENATE	*Candidate*	40.4%	96.4%
	Party/coordinated	25.0%	0.2%
	Interest group	34.6%	3.4%

	Sponsor	Competitive	Uncompetitive
HOUSE	*Candidate*	34.3%	92.1%
	Party/coordinated	48.3%	1.6%
	Interest group	17.4%	6.3%

Sources: The Rothenberg Political Report and Wesleyan Media Project

In Iowa's Senate contest between Joni Ernst and Bruce Braley, for instance, interest groups sponsored 42 percent of total airings between September 1 and Election Day, more than the 29 percent from candidates and 29 percent from parties (including coordinated spots).

Turning to House races, party and coordinated advertising accounted for nearly half of airings (48 percent) in competitive races. Just over a third (34 percent) of ads in competitive races were sponsored by candidates, while interest-group-sponsored airings made up 17 percent of the total. The lower rates of interest-group advertising in 2014 House races is not surprising given that control of that chamber was never in doubt. By contrast, many predicted that control of the Senate could either stay in Democratic hands or fall to the Republicans, and thus interest groups were especially involved in Senate contests.

In sum, the volume of campaign advertising has increased over the past decade, though it has plateaued more recently. This increase, while causing many voters to complain that there are too many ads, also means that there is more information out there for voters to access. But that additional information is not available to all; by and large, only those voters residing in districts with competitive campaigns are being exposed to the deluge of ads. Importantly, many of the ads on television in recent campaigns are ones sponsored by interest groups, which leads to a host of concerns about transparency and the ability of groups to "buy" elections—points we will consider in more depth in future chapters.

TONE OF TELEVISION ADVERTISING

It would be impossible to talk about advertising trends over the last decade and a half without noting trends in tone in particular. As any casual television viewer living in a competitive area knows, election season is synonymous with negative advertising, for good reason: the airwaves are chock-full of attack ads. Raleigh residents who were watching football on Fox on Sunday, October 26, 2014, saw ten different political creatives for North Carolina's Senate race during the commercial breaks, some of which aired multiple times. Only one ad was sponsored by Republican Thom Tillis; two were sponsored by Democratic incumbent Kay Hagan. Three were aired by the National Republican Senatorial Committee (NRSC) on Tillis's behalf, and one was sponsored by the Democratic Senatorial Campaign Committee (DSCC) to benefit Hagan. The final three were sponsored by outside interest groups. Only one of the ten ads was positive, and eight were purely negative.

The sole positive ad was one sponsored by Kay Hagan in which she boasted about being named the most moderate senator by *National Journal*. Sitting at a table in what appeared to be a home, she noted that "one of the things I love about North Carolina is that unless you are talking basketball, you don't have to pick a team. That's how I get results for folks here at home, Republican or Democrat."[4] Challenger

Thom Tillis also spoke directly into the camera in his ad and conveyed his vision of what North Carolina's senator should do. However, his ad also explicitly referenced Hagan, calling her "a rubber stamp for President Obama [who] does everything he wants." Although the ad contained positive elements (for example, a description of his vision for North Carolina), the ad is classified as a contrast ad because it mentioned his opponent.[5]

The remaining eight ads that aired were very different from those two. Most featured ominous music, dark backgrounds or visuals, and plenty of blame. In particular, each laid out a series of problems and pointed to one of the two candidates as the individual responsible. The NRSC ad, for example, accused Kay Hagan of being "what's wrong with Washington." While tense music played in the background, a darkened picture of Hagan appeared on a split screen, which also showed piles of money labeled "Washington's wasteful stimulus." A line skyrocketed up the page while a deep voice continued, "Look at Kay Hagan and Washington's wasteful stimulus. Hagan's family is worth up to fifty million dollars, but a company owned by Hagan's husband used the stimulus to cash in, receiving hundreds of thousands of your tax dollars. The same stimulus Kay Hagan voted for. Hagan sees no conflict of interest. What do *you* think? Kay Hagan doesn't deserve reelection."[6]

Another negative ad, this one sponsored by Women Vote, included brighter colors than the NRSC ad but also played tense music as six different women of varying age and races—all filmed in what appear to be their homes—voiced their concerns about Thom Tillis's record on women's health care. As each woman spoke, onscreen text highlighted her main point and provided a small but legible citation to a source on which the claim was based. An older woman noted, "He passed sweeping abortion restrictions." Another woman noted with emotion, "Tillis opposes affordable access to even basic health care," while yet another continued, "like mammograms and cancer screening." A younger, twentysomething woman closed the ad, confidently saying directly to the camera, "Thom Tillis, we don't need you making our health care decisions."[7] As all these examples indicate, although viewers tuned in to watch football, they got a large dose of mostly negative messages about the state of affairs in North Carolina and the politicians seeking election.

These examples are not unique. The Wesleyan Media Project and the Wisconsin Advertising Project before it have tracked trends in tone since 1998—the Wisconsin project until 2008; the WMP since 2010. Each unique ad that airs is viewed and classified into one of three mutually exclusive categories: (1) a **positive ad**, sometimes also referred to as a promotional ad, which focuses solely on the favored candidate (for example, the Hagan ad); (2) a **negative ad**, sometimes also referred to as an attack ad, which talks solely about the opposing candidate save for the "paid for by" line (for example, the NRSC and Women Vote ads); or (3) a **contrast ad**, which mentions both the favored and opposing candidate (for example, the Tillis ad). As shown clearly in Figure 3.4, negative ads in the general election have been increasing since 2000, rising in congressional races from just under 20 percent of airings in 2000 to the majority in 2014. In the 2012 presidential race, nearly two out of every three ads were negative.

Citizens and journalists alike frequently decry the amount of negativity on the airwaves during elections, and Figure 3.4 indicates that their complaints are not without cause. Negativity has been increasing over the past decade, so much so that negativity is now the dominant form of advertising in elections. It is worth noting that although negativity has clearly increased in recent elections, it doesn't necessarily follow that that today's campaigns are the most negative in history. The data analyzed here go back only as far as 1998.

As effectively conveyed in the satirical video "Attack Ads, Circa 1800," written and produced by *Reason* magazine, campaigning in the 1800s was anything but civil.[8] For example, John Adams was called "blind, bald, crippled, toothless," while another newspaper warned that with Thomas Jefferson as president, "murder, robbery, rape, adultery, and incest will be openly taught and practiced, the air will be rent with the cries of the distressed, the soil will be soaked with blood, and the nation [will be] black with crimes." In comparison to these statements, today's negative campaigning and the negative ads described

Figure 3.4: Percentage of Negative Advertising over Time in the Top 75 Markets, September 1–Election Day of Each Year

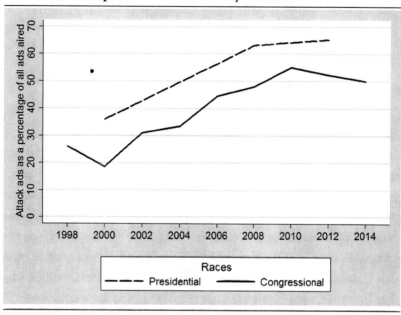

Sources: Wisconsin Advertising Project and Wesleyan Media Project

above may seem downright civil—though not necessarily any more appetizing to the American public.

Which brings us to a central question: if citizens universally report disliking negativity, why are there record numbers of negative ads on the air? Again, the answer has to do with both the competitiveness of the races and the stakes involved. Table 3.5 compares the tone of the ads in competitive Senate races to those in races deemed to be solidly in one party's camp in 2012. As we already know, the volume of advertising for uncompetitive races is much lower than for competitive ones; advertising for uncompetitive races is also overwhelmingly positive, to the tune of over 80 percent.

In contrast, fewer than two out of every ten ads in competitive races are positive. Negativity reigns in those races, with attack ads constituting 61 percent of the ads on the air while contrast spots, which often feel just as negative, making up an additional 22 percent. Clearly,

Table 3.5: Tone in 2012 Senate Race Ads by Competitiveness, September 1–Election Day

	Competitive	Uncompetitive
Positive	16.9%	80.6%
Contrast	22.0%	9.8%
Negative	61.1%	9.6%

Sources: Wesleyan Media Project and Roll Call

competition changes the air war into an offensive battle in which both sides believe that negativity is an important tactic in moving voters in their favor. Evidence from political science supports this view, finding that negative advertising can reduce positive feelings toward targeted candidates[9] and may be especially important for challengers, given the inherent benefits of incumbency.[10] There is also evidence to suggest that citizens are more attentive to negative information,[11] which further incentivizes campaigns to use negative ads as a persuasive tool.

It is also important to recognize that different advertising sponsors have different incentives with respect to tone. As you can see in Table 3.6, candidates are far more likely to air positive ads than are parties and interest groups. This makes sense: while negativity has been shown to lower the favorability of the targeted candidate, it also carries the risk of **backlash**, meaning that the sponsor of a negative ad can also suffer a decline in favorability after airing an attack.[12] Plus, most campaigns see value in promoting their candidates positively, given that roughly a third of candidate-sponsored airings are positive ones. Still, candidates do not completely shy away from negativity. As shown in the table, nearly four out of ten candidate-sponsored airings in 2012 were negative in tone, indicating that candidates do sometimes perceive the benefits of "going negative" as outweighing the risks.

However, as you can see in Table 3.6, interest groups and parties are far more likely to air negative ads than candidates. That parties and interest groups serve as the "attack dogs" for candidates makes sense when one considers the American public's dislike of negative advertising. Negative ads sponsored by parties and, especially, interest

Table 3.6: Tone in 2012 Federal Race Ads by Sponsor, September 1–Election Day

Sponsor	Positive	Contrast	Negative
Candidate	32.5%	28.5%	39.0%
Party/coordinated	4.5%	17.2%	78.3%
Interest group	5.9%	11.0%	83.1%

Source: Wesleyan Media Project

groups have been demonstrated to shield candidates from the backlash that would occur if they were to sponsor the negative ads themselves.[13] Therefore, the increasing negativity in campaigns may be due in part to the increasing number of ads aired by interest groups.

Although negativity may draw citizen ire, it is not inherently bad, and in fact it plays a very important role in campaigns. More specifically, negativity has been shown to stimulate citizen interest[14] and to boost knowledge, particularly among citizens who initially know less about politics.[15] This may be because negative ads generally contain more substantive information than positive ones.[16] This may seem counterintuitive at first, but it becomes clearer as we consider concrete examples of positive and negative ads.

There are several types of positive ads, but the stereotypical positive ad is a biographical one designed to introduce you to the candidate and convince you that he or she is a regular person, someone who works hard, has a supportive family, and will represent your interests faithfully. We've all seen these ads—more often than not, the candidate (particularly if male) appears in a blue shirt and khaki pants, smiling and walking through a park with his family. And almost invariably, as our mentor, Ken Goldstein, used to joke, a yellow Labrador makes an appearance to secure the desired "dog lover" vote.

In the 2010 senatorial race in Wisconsin, Republican challenger Ron Johnson aired an ad intended to poke fun at this genre of positive advertising (see Figure 3.5a). The ad was set in a home and showed Johnson standing with his wife and three children. All five turned to smile at the camera while an overly upbeat voice said, "Introducing the Ron Johnson family!" The family members took turns praising Johnson in ways that showcase how "normal" they are: Ben, the son, looked at his phone while he said in a monotone, "He's a great role model." Jenna, one of the daughters, squinted at the camera and slowly stated, as if she were reading a cue card, "He's worked extremely hard all his life." At the end, while his family laughed, Johnson said, "Obviously I'm not a professional politician and they are not professional actors. We're just a Wisconsin family worried about our country. I'm Ron Johnson, and I approve this message because it's time to get our nation's house in order."[17]

The ad satirized the positive-ad stereotype but failed to overcome it. Little policy information was conveyed in the ad, and viewers were left with no idea where Johnson stood on the important issues of the day, such as health care reform or how best to boost the economy. This is where negative and contrast advertising have a distinct advantage. They're specifically intended to draw attention to the issues, and evidence suggests that negative ads are more likely to be about substantive issues than personal characteristics (though they do sometimes focus on the flaws in a candidate's character).

Contrast the satirical Johnson ad described above with the negative one he sponsored during that same campaign (see Figure 3.5b). The ad started with an image of then incumbent Senator Russ Feingold and a voiceover: "The guy named Russ Feingold was the number-one maverick and independent in the entire United States Senate." The screen then froze and split. On the left side of the screen, bolded words appeared to highlight the woman's voiceover, as she said, "Not really. Feingold went along with all the other mavericks for the government takeover of health care. He fell in line along with all the other mavericks voting for the failed stimulus, and he was really maverick-y when it came time to increase the debt limit. Let's get serious. Russ Feingold a maverick? Not anymore. He votes the party line." In contrast to the positive ad, this spot contained lots of substantive information about Feingold's voting history in the Senate, giving the viewer a clear idea of where he stood on the issues (obviously not in a flattering way, since this was an ad sponsored by Johnson).[18]

Figure 3.5a: Ron Johnson's 2010 "The Johnson Family" Ad for Senate

Source: Courtesy of the Ron Johnson for Senate campaign

Figure 3.5b: Ron Johnson's 2010 "Maverick" Ad for Senate

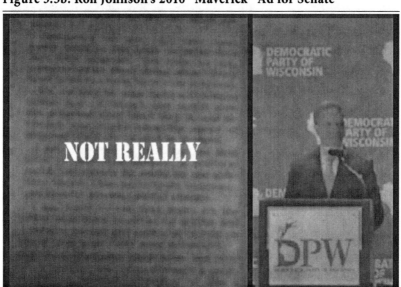

Source: Courtesy of the Ron Johnson for Senate campaign

Clearly, negative and especially contrast ads are typically anything but fluff. They highlight real or perceived differences between candidates on the issues and convey that something important is at stake, and they often use appeals to fear or anger to make their point. With that in mind, it is probably not surprising that studies find negative ads to be more memorable than positive ads. Appeals to fear may even induce viewers to seek out more information,[19] and in a world where citizens often tune out politics, a little fear can do some good in terms of increasing the electorate's information base. We will return to these themes in future chapters.

Although much of the scholarly evidence on negative ads suggests that their role is important and even democratically desirable, there are some caveats and exceptions. One potentially troubling new area of research on negative ads has to do with the rise and influence of interest groups, especially newer interest groups such as 501c organizations and super PACs. A small but growing body of literature suggests that negative advertising from unknown groups may be more effective than negative ads from candidates[20] and even parties.[21] There are two potential reasons for this: The first is that, as already discussed, interest groups help to shield candidates from the backlash that would occur for airing negative ads, and since the goal is change in *candidate* favorability, the net effect of the ad (persuasion minus backlash) is higher. The second reason is that most of these groups have names that are not well known but sound "all-American"—Patriot Majority, Americans for Prosperity, and Independence USA, to name a few. Citizens tend to see candidates (and even parties to some extent) as self-interested (that is, concerned only about winning votes, at any cost), whereas little-known interest groups with names that prime values of patriotism, independence, or prosperity, for example, don't necessarily carry the same stigma.

Ironically, although citizens do not necessarily know the group or its party affiliation, they tend to view messages from these all-American-sounding organizations as more credible than those from candidates. That their ads are viewed as more credible than candidate and party ads—and thus are generally more effective—may encourage the formation of even more interest groups that raise money and spend it on political ads. This could result in several outcomes, some good and some bad. One is more campaign negativity, as interest groups overwhelmingly engage in this type of advertising. Although they would likely decry it, voters might actually benefit from this outcome because they would have more information to use in making their voting decisions. Second, the growth of interest-group-sponsored advertising might also help to blunt partisan polarization: because people do not instantly recognize the group's name or identify the message as partisan, these ads can cut through partisan predispositions to reach those who usually favor the opposing side. A third outcome is the waning of transparency, as voters will know less about who is sponsoring the ads they see on television, especially if the new groups organize as dark money groups. Finally, given their lack of transparency and accountability, interest groups may have more incentive to stretch the truth in their ads. Thus, the additional information that voters might receive from negative interest-group-sponsored ads must be weighed against the possibility that the information is more unreliable than information contained in candidate-sponsored ads.

ISSUES IN TELEVISION ADVERTISING

Now that we have discussed the volume and tone of political advertising, let us turn our attention to what these ads are actually about—that is, the issues they cover and how they align with Americans' concerns. Although candidates are prone to focus on the issues that play to their strengths, their messages are most likely to resonate when those issues also align with citizens' concerns. As such, we should expect advertising to correspond with the issues most Americans view as most important. According to Gallup, in late 2010 roughly two-thirds of Americans cited economic issues as the nation's most important problem. That percentage dropped 50 percent by the end of 2014, to just over a third.[22] Table 3.7 confirms this expectation, showing that in 2010, both pro-Democrat and pro-Republican airings for House and

Senate races were most likely to mention employment and jobs. While these issues did not go away in the 2014 midterms, they did drop in frequency from the most highlighted issue to the number-two spot for both parties. The percentage of airings mentioning employment and jobs drops from 39 percent to 18 percent for pro-Democrat airings and from 50.5 percent to 23 percent for pro-Republican airings.

Because the American public had become less focused on the economic recession of 2008 and no dominant issue rose to take its place in the public mind, the 2014 election was a midterm without a theme (or perhaps one with many themes). This is reflected in the data in Table 3.7. No single issue dominated the ad airings for Republicans or Democrats in 2014. You can also see the ebb and flow of the public's attention to other issues, such as foreign affairs, in the number of campaign ad mentions. For example, while foreign policy topics (broadly conceived) received less than 2 percent of issues mentions in 1998 and 2000, they constituted a much greater share of references in advertising following the September 11 attacks and grew even more once the war in Iraq got underway.[23]

To what extent do candidates—and parties and interest groups, for that matter—discuss the same issues or focus on different topics altogether? There is evidence to suggest that as the number of ads increases and the competitiveness of the race increases, there is more **issue convergence** (when competitors discuss the same set of issues) in political advertising.[24] Many view issue convergence as a positive, as it allows voters to compare opposing candidates on the same issues—it's much easier to see clear differences between candidates if one mentions supporting an increased minimum wage and the other mentions eliminating it, than if one mentions supporting an increased minimum wage and the other mentions opposing a free trade agreement. Issue convergence, then, can make voters' choices clearer. Of course, such positive effects may be contingent on an honest and clear discussion of the topic. Voters may not benefit if competing candidates merely mention the same issue in vague terms and fail to actually engage each other.[25]

Table 3.7: Top Issues by Party in US House and Senate Race Ads, September 1–Election Day

2010 MIDTERMS			
Pro-Democrat Ads		**Pro-Republican Ads**	
Employment/jobs	38.7%	Employment/jobs	50.5%
Taxes	34.9%	Taxes	41.5%
Trade/globalization	17.9%	Gov't spending	39.9%
Social Security	15.3%	Deficit/budget/debt	34.9%
China	9.7%	Health care	33.6%
Health care	8.7%	Recession/Stimulus	31.5%

2014 MIDTERMS			
Pro-Democrat Ads		**Pro-Republican Ads**	
Taxes	26.3%	ACA/Obamacare	27.6%
Employment/jobs	17.7%	Employment/jobs	23.3%
Medicare	17.2%	Taxes	19.4%
Social Security	16.1%	Deficit/budget/debt	16.8%
Education/schools	15.2%	Medicare	12.9%
Veterans	9.9%	Gov't spending	12.5%

Source: Wesleyan Media Project. Percentages for each party in each year can add up to more than 100 because ads often mention more than one issue.

CONCLUSION

This chapter has shown that the volume of advertising has been on the rise since 2000, reaching a high-water mark in the past couple of election cycles. More ads means more information for voters to use when making up their minds—not necessarily a bad thing. We suspect, however, that the massive rises in the volume of television advertising each election cycle are unlikely to continue. Even though it is easier to get money into the political system than in the past, advertisers are becoming smarter, spreading their advertising dollars among television, radio, print, and the Internet.

One reason for the rise in ad volumes is the increased role of interest groups, who, as we noted in Chapter 2, can raise large sums of money quite easily and have virtually no restrictions on what they can say in their ads. Yet interest groups direct most of the advertising dollars into a few highly competitive races. That groups are sponsoring a much greater share of the ads on television is concerning to some given that groups lack the accountability that candidates have; that is, you cannot vote against a group whose ad makes you angry as you can a candidate. Some candidates are also concerned that groups are "hijacking" the issue agenda, getting voters to focus on issues the candidates don't want to talk about. This can be good if those issues are ones that are important and matter to voters, but it can make it difficult for candidates to control their own messages.

Since 2000, advertising has also become more negative. Interest groups are also responsible, at least in part, for this trend, as groups do not experience the voter backlash that candidates do when they run negative ads, and thus the vast majority of ads aired by groups are negative. More negative ads means more ads that talk about policy, which is presumably useful to voters, but it also can lead to voter complaints and campaigns in which voters never really get introduced to the candidates as humans and what passions drive their run for office.

Finally, this chapter revealed that while many ads do talk about issues, what gets discussed varies considerably depending on what citizens believe are the most important issues facing the country. In a sense, then, campaigns are responsive to voters, talking about the issues that they want to hear about. But how much citizens actually gain from this issue discussion remains an open question.

NOTES

1. See especially: John Zaller, *The Nature and Origins of Mass Opinion,* Cambridge Studies in Public Opinion and Political Psychology (Cambridge, UK: Cambridge University Press, 1992); William J. McGuire, "The Myth of Massive Media Impact: Savagings and Salvagings," in *Public Communication and Behavior,* ed. George Comstock (Orlando, FL: Academic Press, 1986), 1: 173–257.

DISCUSSION QUESTIONS

1. Why do interest groups and parties run far more ads in competitive races than in uncompetitive races? Why does this pattern hold true even for candidates?

2. Why do interest groups run more negative ads than candidates do? How does the competitiveness of the race influence how negative the advertising is? Why?

3. Is the rise of interest-group advertising concerning to you? Why or why not?

4. The benefits of negativity depend on the claims in ads being true. Sponsors of ads certainly may stretch the truth or even lie. How do we handle this possibility? That is, what might incentivize ad sponsors to make only truthful claims?

2. Travis N. Ridout and Michael M. Franz, *The Persuasive Power of Campaign Advertising* (Philadelphia, PA: Temple University Press, 2011); Michael M. Franz, "Interest Groups in Electoral Politics: 2012 in Context," *The Forum: A Journal of Applied Research in Contemporary Politics* 10, no. 4 (2012): 62–79.

3. We considered ads whose content was slightly modified for different states to be a single instance of a creative.

4. https://www.youtube.com/watch?v=Y4OQZ1I6xVg.

5. https://www.youtube.com/watch?v=fkcUDPnYvFY.

6. https://www.youtube.com/watch?v=2Z7vdN89jhU.

7. https://www.youtube.com/watch?v=smNo4Ll_4Yg.

8. Meredith Bragg, writer and producer, "Attack Ads, Circa 1800," *Hit and Run Blog, Reason.com*, video, 1 minute 43 seconds, October 29, 2010, http://reason.com/blog/2010/10/29/attack-ads-circa-1800.

9. Kim Leslie Fridkin and Patrick J. Kenney, "Do Negative Messages Work? The Impact of Negativity on Citizens' Evaluations of Candidates," *American Politics Research* 32, no. 5 (September 2004): 570–605; Travis N. Ridout, Michael M. Franz, and Erika Franklin Fowler, "Sponsorship, Disclosure and Donors: Limiting the Impact of Outside Group Ads," *Political Research Quarterly* 68, no. 1 (March 2015): 154–166.

10. Richard R. Lau and Gerald Pomper, *Negative Campaigning: An Analysis of U.S. Senate Elections* (Lanham, MD: Rowman and Littlefield, 2004); Ridout and Franz, *The Persuasive Power of Campaign Advertising*.

11. Stuart Soroka and Stephen McAdams, "News, Politics, and Negativity," *Political Communication*, 32, no. 1 (2015): 1–22.

12. Gina M. Garramone, "Effects of Negative Political Advertising: The Roles of Sponsor and Rebuttal," *Journal of Broadcasting and Electronic Media* 29, no. 2 (1985): 147–159; Brian L. Roddy, and Gina M. Garramone, "Appeals and Strategies of Negative Political Advertising," *Journal of Broadcasting and Electronic Media* 32, no. 4: 415–427.

13. Deborah Jordan Brooks and Michael Murov, "Assessing Accountability in a Post–*Citizens United* Era: The Effects of Attack Ad Sponsorship by Unknown Independent Groups," *American Politics Research* 40, no. 3 (2012): 383–418; Conor M. Dowling and Amber Wichowsky, "Attacks Without Consequence? Candidates, Parties, Groups, and the Changing Face of Negative Advertising," *American Journal of Political Science* 59, no. 1 (2015): 19–36.

14. Larry M. Bartels, "Partisanship and Voting Behavior, 1952–1996," *American Journal of Political Science* 44, no. 1 (January 2000): 35–50; Ted Brader, *Campaigning for Hearts and Minds: How Emotional Appeals in Political Ads Work* (Chicago: University of Chicago Press, 2006); George E. Marcus, W. R. Neuman, and M. MacKuen, *Affective Intelligence and Political Judgment* (Chicago: University of Chicago Press, 2000).

15. Michael M. Franz, Paul Freedman, Ken Goldstein, and Travis N. Ridout, *Campaign Advertising and American Democracy* (Philadelphia, PA: Temple University Press, 2007); Travis N. Ridout, Dhavan Shah, Ken Goldstein, and Michael M. Franz, "Evaluating Measures of Campaign Advertising Exposure on Political Learning," *Political Behavior* 26, no. 3 (September 2004): 201–225.

16. John G. Geer, *In Defense of Negativity: Attack Ads in Presidential Campaigns* (Chicago: University of Chicago Press, 2006); Franz, Freedman, Goldstein, and Ridout, *Campaign Advertising and American Democracy*.

17. Dean Robbins. "Ron Johnson Fakes It in 'The Johnson Family' Ad," *Isthmus*, September 9, 2010, http://www.isthmus.com/opinion/ron-johnson-fakes-it -in-the-johnson-family-ad/.

18. "WI-Sen: Johnson Ad: 'Russ Feingold a Maverick? Not Anymore," *Real Clear Politics*, October 27, 2010, http://www.realclearpolitics.com/video/2010/10 /27/wi-sen_johnson_ad_russ_feingold_a_maverick_not_anymore.html.

19. Brader, *Campaigning for Hearts and Minds*.

20. Brooks and Murov, "Assessing Accountability in a Post–*Citizens United* Era"; Tyler Johnson, Johanna Dunaway, and Christopher R. Weber, "Consider the Source: Variations in the Effects of Negative Campaign Messages," *Journal of Integrated Social Sciences* 2, no. 1 (2011): 98–127; Ridout, Franz, and Fowler, "Sponsorship, Disclosure and Donors."

21. Dowling and Wichowsky, "Attacks Without Consequence?"

22. Gallup, "Most Important Problem," In-Depth: Topics A to Z, 2015, http://www.gallup.com/poll/1675/most-important-problem.aspx.

23. Travis N. Ridout, Michael M. Franz, and Erika Franklin Fowler, "Advances in the Study of Political Advertising," *Journal of Political Marketing* 13, no. 3 (2014): 175–194.

24. Franz, "Interest Groups in Electoral Politics."

25. Keena Lipsitz, "Issue Convergence Is Nothing More than Issue Convergence," *Political Research Quarterly* 66, no. 4 (2013): 843–855.

CHAPTER 4

How Ads Are Created and Tested

The "Stage" ad started with film of railroad tracks and a factory. It then transitioned to Mike Earnest, a blue-collar worker from Indiana, who explained: "Out of the blue one day, we were told to build a thirty-foot stage. Gathered the guys, and we built that thirty-foot stage, not knowing what it was for." Earnest continued, "Just days later, all three shifts were told to assemble in the warehouse. A group of people walked out on that stage, and told us that the plant is now closed, and all of you are fired. I looked both ways, I looked at the crowd, and we all just lost our jobs. We don't have an income."

Who was responsible for the plant's closing down? The ad, aired by Priorities USA, a super PAC founded by former Obama campaign managers, pinned the blame on the 2012 Republican presidential nominee, Mitt Romney, whose company, Bain Capital, had purchased the factory. As Earnest put it, "Mitt Romney made over a hundred million dollars by shutting down our plant and devastated our lives. Turns out that when we built that stage, it was like building my own coffin. And it just made me sick."[1]

This ad was one of the most effective ads of the 2012 presidential campaign. How do we know that? It's not just the judgments of political pundits that attest to the ad's effectiveness; there are data from ad testing and focus groups to back up the claim. One firm that does ad testing is Ace Metrix. During the 2012 presidential campaign, the firm

Figure 4.1: Priorities USA Action's 2012 "Stage" Ad Attacking Mitt Romney

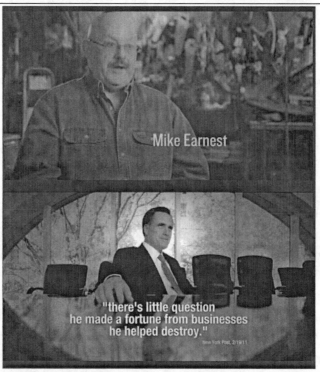

Source: Courtesy of Priorities USA Action

tested over three hundred unique ads during the primary and general election seasons through online surveys, showing each of them to a five-hundred-person sample that was representative of the population of the United States. The participants were asked to evaluate how credible, memorable, informative, and persuasive the ad was, as well as the likelihood that they would watch the ad again under different viewing conditions, such as when watching a favorite television program or channel surfing. Ace Metrix then combined these answers to create an effectiveness score for each ad that ranges from 1 to 950.

The "Stage" ad came out on top among independent voters with a score of 562, no doubt in part due to the heartfelt personal story Mike Earnest told directly into the camera and the powerful images of small, middle-class homes and empty buildings. Another ad that scored highly among independent voters was one from the Obama campaign called "Mosaic" that also highlighted the theme of economic populism. It discussed Romney's record as governor of Massachusetts—how he had cut taxes on millionaires but raised hundreds of other fees and taxes on small items. One anti-Obama ad that was particularly effective was sponsored by the group Let Freedom Ring. The sixty-second ad featured ordinary people discussing how the price of gas had increased significantly during Obama's presidency.

These are examples of effective ads, but there is also an important point to be made about how they were crafted. Before these ads ever appeared on the air, the campaigns and their consultants made several decisions about their content, and these decisions were shaped by much research and analysis. In other words, the ads you see on television, especially in high-profile races such as those for president or governor, were carefully developed, designed, and tested. This chapter will discuss the decisions that campaigns make regarding the content of ads—and the tools used to test the effectiveness of those ads.

THE ELEMENTS OF A POLITICAL AD

Political ads are all about creating a particular mood that helps to convey the ad's message. Ad makers are well aware that both the message and the mood can be set by altering the ad's features, including its length, tone, visual images and color, voiceover and music, and for candidates the federally mandated approval line.

Length

Most political ads that air on television in the United States are thirty seconds long, though a small percentage are fifteen or sixty seconds long. In very rare instances, ads can be even longer: in late October 2012, the Obama campaign produced a thirty-minute infomercial that aired simultaneously on three broadcast television networks and some cable networks. Ads that are three or five minutes long are more common in countries like Britain, which provides free airtime to political parties. And of course, online-only ads that are never shown on television do not have to conform to television stations' standard commercial lengths and therefore vary considerably in length.

Ads that are a mere fifteen seconds long are less costly than thirty-second ads, so they are sometimes used when raising name recognition is especially important or when the campaign wants to convey one very simple message. But fifteen seconds is very little time in which to convey information, and that means there's less chance to grab viewers' attention and make them think about the ad's message.

Campaigns tend to stick to thirty-second ads as a function of convention and cost considerations. Americans are used to seeing thirty-second commercials, and advertisers tend to find that they can convey an effective message about an issue in that amount of time. However, if advertisers have the funds, it is not uncommon for them to air a political ad first as a sixty-second commercial to get the full message across and then to repeat the ad in condensed, thirty-second versions to reiterate the initial point.

Tone

Scholars typically divide ads into three tone categories. As noted in Chapter 3, negative ads are those that mention an opponent or the unsupported candidate, positive ads only mention the ad's sponsor or the favored candidate, and contrast ads mention both candidates. If we look at the ads aired in 2014 between January 1 and Election Day in races for Senate, House, and governor, we find that about 39 percent were positive, 21 percent were contrast ads, and 40 percent were negative.

Although dividing ads into three tone categories based on who is mentioned is fairly easy to do, it does have a drawback: some ads that "feel" negative to viewers—they have dark images and ominous music designed to scare us—are still labeled "positive" if they do not mention an opponent. Indeed, one of the most famous "negative" ads in history would be considered positive by this definition because no opponent is mentioned. The "Daisy Girl" ad, aired by President Lyndon Johnson's campaign in 1964, featured a young girl counting as she plucked petals from a flower (see Figure 4.2). The viewer then heard a narrator

Figure 4.2: Lyndon Johnson's "Daisy Girl" Ad from 1964

Source: Courtesy Democratic National Committee

begin counting down a rocket launch and saw a bomb explode. The implication was that nuclear war was imminent if you voted for Barry Goldwater, Johnson's Republican opponent, but Goldwater's name was never mentioned.[2]

Campaigns often use positive ads early in a campaign in order to introduce voters to the candidate. Many campaigns produce a biographical piece that may feature the candidate and his or her happy family (dogs included) and reveal a bit about the candidate's experience. In recent years, however, campaigns have also employed negative ads relatively early in the election season in order to define opponents before they can define themselves. In August 2004, just as many voters were beginning to pay attention to the general election race, a group called Swift Boat Veterans for Truth ran an ad in several battleground states that accused Democratic nominee John Kerry of lying about his military heroism as a soldier in Vietnam. Another good example of this strategy was the Obama campaign's portrayal of Mitt Romney as an out-of-touch rich guy in the 2012 campaign. In addition to the "Stage" ad, which aired in May 2012, another ad that aired in July highlighted Romney's bank accounts in tax havens like Bermuda and the Cayman Islands. These negative ads came at a time when Romney was relatively short on cash and thus unable to define himself through advertising.

Visual Images and Color

The visual imagery used in political ads can play an important role in conveying who a candidate is, or at least the image the candidate wants to project. Many candidates, for instance, try to burnish their image as patriots by including an image of an American flag. In 2014, just over one in four political ads contained an American flag. The flag was even more common in positive ads, appearing in almost one in three.

The visual images in an ad can also convey policy stances. In 2014, many candidates were pictured holding—and firing—guns.[3] This tells the viewer that the candidate supports Second Amendment rights and may, more subtly, portray the candidate as a fighter frustrated with the status quo in government. For instance, in Montana, congressional candidate Matt Rosendale fired at an alleged "government drone" in one ad. In Washington state, Democratic congressional candidate Estakio Beltran fired at an elephant-shaped piñata, which presumably represented the Republican Party. And a memorable ad that aired in Iowa showed Senate candidate Joni Ernst wearing a black leather jacket and riding her Harley as the narrator described her as a "mom, farm girl, and a lieutenant colonel who carries more than just lipstick in her purse." The scene then shifted to a firing range, where Ernst took several shots at a target. As the narrator explained, "Once she sets her sights on Obamacare, Joni's going to unload."

Imagery can also be used to tap into local sentiments. For example, in the 2012 campaign, Barack Obama aired four different versions of his "Higher Education" ad in North Carolina, Nevada, Ohio, and Virginia. The ads were identical in text and music, but they each had different imagery in the middle that was taken from college campuses in each state, intended to be recognizable to residents of that state.

A related major element in political advertising is color. As political scientist Darrell West discovered,[4] bright colors are used to associate positivity with a candidate while dark colors are used to associate negativity with an opponent. If an opponent is pictured in the ad, campaigns frequently use a low-quality, grainy, black-and-white photo in an attempt to make that person look more ominous. And, of course, campaigns try to find the worst possible photos of opponents to use, ones in which the candidate has a scowl on his or her face and looks particularly unflattering. In a very real way, campaign ads use color to try to tap the image of the conquering hero versus the shady and untrustworthy villain.

Voiceover and Music

The unseen voiceover announcer or narrator is another important element in a political ad. Most political ads in the United States employ a voiceover announcer, usually an experienced voice actor. About 77 percent of ads in 2014 contained a voiceover. Interestingly, male announcers were much more common than female: among those ads that used a voiceover, 32 percent were voiced by women, 60 percent were voiced by men, and 8 percent were voiced by both men and women. Although ad makers tend to default to using men to voice ads—perhaps just because that's the way they have always done it—there are certain circumstances in which the choice of the voiceover announcer is connected to an ad's message. For instance, one rule of thumb is that women should voice ads about so-called women's issues, such as education, child care, and abortion. This may help the ad better connect with women viewers, at whom such ads are generally aimed. There is also a tendency for ad makers to use women to voice negative ads.[5] The idea is that using a woman to voice an attack may tone down the attack and reduce the likelihood that voters will be angry at the ad's sponsor for going negative.

Almost all political ads—98 percent of those aired in 2014—employ background music. The use of music helps to establish an emotional connection with the audience and to convey the tone of the ad, whether positive or negative. As such, it is not surprising that the use of different types of music correlate with tone. We found that 71 percent of negative ads employed music that could be characterized as ominous or tense and about 87 percent of positive ads featured uplifting music. Most contrast ads (83 percent) featured more than one type of music, employing ominous music when speaking about the opponent but transitioning to uplifting music when speaking about the favored candidate.

Approval Line

The final element of a political ad is what is known as the "stand by your ad" requirement. Since the Bipartisan Campaign Reform Act went into effect in late 2002, candidates for federal office (the US Senate, the US House, and the presidency) have been required to personally authorize or approve their campaign's television ads. The idea behind this requirement, which was inserted into the bill by Representative David Price of North Carolina, was that it would make candidates hesitate before airing negative ads, as candidates would not want to associate themselves so closely with attacks. On that front, the requirement was a failure. Chapter 3 already discussed increasing levels of campaign negativity, and more importantly, candidate use of negative and contrast ads in congressional contests did not decrease immediately after BCRA[6] and, if anything, appear to have increased slightly to roughly half of all candidate airings in 2006 and beyond.

Campaigns have come up with creative ways to satisfy the "stand by your ad" requirement. In 2014, House candidate Elise Stefanik made an attempt at humor, patting the head of a cow and saying, "I'm Elise Stefanik, and we approved this message." Illinois Representative Cheri Bustos tried to insert policy in her authorization, stating, "I'm Cheri Bustos, and I approved this message because the American flag should be made right here in America." In Louisiana, Senator Mary Landrieu made the approval a central part of one of her ads. After she started the ad by stating, "I'm Mary Landrieu, and I approved this message," her father, politician Moon Landrieu, turned to her and asked, "Don't you say that at the end?" Mary Landrieu explained, knowing her father was going to shower praise on her, "You can start with it . . . I'm not so sure I want to approve it at the end of this."[7]

When the sponsor of the ad is a group, such as the National Rifle Association or Crossroads GPS, then no candidate approval is required. Indeed, such groups are legally barred from coordinating with candidates when creating their ad messages. Groups must, however, reveal both verbally (usually through a voiceover) and visually (in a "paid for by" line) that they are responsible for the ad. The same disclaimer requirements hold for political parties that pay for ads with independent expenditures. Interestingly, however, while disclaimers are required for television, radio, and print ads—even billboards—it is only required for online ads that sponsors pay to appear on another website.

MAKING THE AD

Making a political ad can be a multistep process, though the exact number of steps involved varies depending on the sophistication of the campaign and how much time the campaign has available. Dennis W. Johnson, a professor who has written extensively about how to run a political campaign, outlined the steps in the process of making a political ad: research and ad concept, ad creation, ad testing, and final production and launch.[8]

Research and Ad Concept

Often the first step in making a political ad is research. Johnson suggests that campaigns rely upon four different types of research: (1) a benchmark survey, (2) a targeting analysis, (3) focus group studies, and finally, (4) interviews with the candidates and their family and friends along with background investigation into the candidate's characteristics, experiences, and accomplishments. All of this information helps to address the central question: what about this candidate, whether personal characteristics or issue stances, can we emphasize to attract the group of voters we want to attract?

A **benchmark survey** is an initial survey of voters that provides the campaign with information on how much (if anything) voters already know about the candidate in question and how they feel about particular issues and themes likely to be used in the campaign. For example, in 2012, Mitt Romney's campaign would have been interested in figuring out how much voters knew about his business success and how they felt about budget discipline, particularly given the recent financial crisis.

A **targeting analysis** is a way of identifying who already supports the candidate and which subgroups might be persuadable. Romney's campaign found that most strong Republicans and male businessmen were already supporters of Mitt Romney. Women, especially those without strong political affiliations, were a key population the campaign identified as one they needed to target for votes.

Focus groups are gatherings of generally seven to twelve people who engage in a conversation guided by a moderator about a particular topic. Focus groups are particularly important in developing ad messages that work. For instance, in 2012, Republican strategists used focus groups to identify ways to talk about budget deficits that would appeal to politically independent women.[9] Republicans found that the best way to reach these women was to frame the prolonged deficit as a problem that their children would inherit. As a result of this research, the Romney campaign aired an ad that started with the image of a baby held by her mother, hammering home the idea that the burden of the deficit would fall on the innocent, defenseless next generation (see Figure 4.3). The female narrator (of course) said, "Dear daughter, your share of Obama's debt is over fifty thousand dollars, and it grows every day." This ad also stands out for the marked contrast between tone and imagery: even though it is negative in tone, the soft lighting and the sympathetic image of a mother with her baby is far from the usual grainy lighting, dark colors, and ominous music that characterize negative ads.[10] On the Democratic side in 2014, responses from focus groups led Democrats to make wealthy businessmen and political donors Charles

Figure 4.3: Mitt Romney's 2012 "Dear Daughter" Ad Attacking Obama on Federal Debt

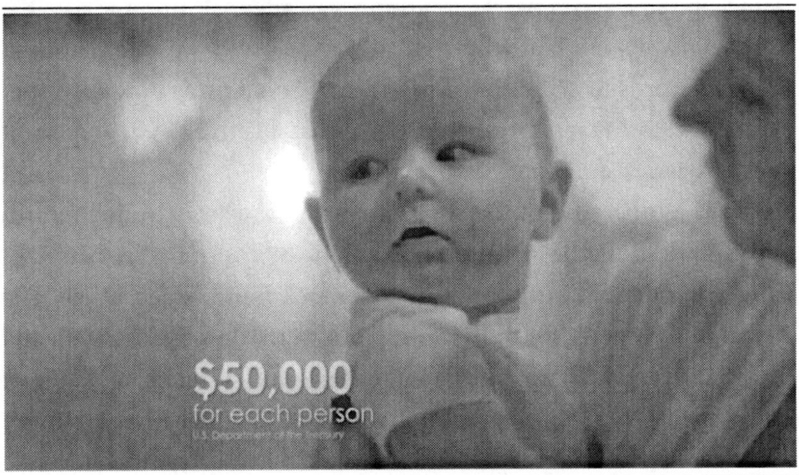

$50,000
for each person
U.S. Department of the Treasury

Source: Courtesy of Romney for President, Inc.

and David Koch's support for Republican candidates an issue in several ads. In one ad in Louisiana, the Democratic-leaning group Senate Majority PAC referred to the Koch brothers as "out-of-state billionaires." In Michigan, one of the group's ads displayed a picture of the brothers above that of Republican candidate Terri Lynn Land.

What message to convey in an ad is typically decided by a senior media consultant with input from others on the campaign, including pollsters and the candidate. But regardless of who the decision maker is, the content of the ad's message is informed by the research done earlier and the group or groups of voters to whom the campaign wants to speak.

Ad Creation

How much time and money is needed for ad creation can vary considerably. At one end of the scale are quickly made ads whose production involves nothing more than someone sitting at a computer manipulating stock photos and adding a voiceover and music. These relatively unsophisticated, rapid-response ads are meant to be web-only and are not shown on television. In May 2012, Democrat Cory Booker, now a senator from New Jersey, criticized President Obama's attacks on Bain Capital, the company that Romney headed. Within the day, the Romney campaign had a new video posted on its website that used Booker's words to criticize the president.[11] Some firms now even specialize in creating rapid-response ads so that no attack by an opponent goes unanswered.

At the other end of the spectrum are ads whose production involves extensive filming and production. In 2000, for instance, Al Gore's presidential campaign filmed a mock music video titled "The Ballad of George W. Bush." Filming took place on a Texas ranch and involved twenty cast and crew members, twenty vehicles, and at least one camel.[12] In 2004, Representative David Wu was filmed bungee jumping off of a bridge.[13]

Many ads aired by candidates for federal office fall somewhere in the middle of these two extremes. It takes time to arrange a location for filming a candidate, and indeed, some candidates get in trouble for filming in places they should not. A congressional candidate in North Dakota, Kevin Cramer, violated cemetery rules in 2014 when he filmed an ad in a veterans cemetery that prohibits filming of political spots, which led to his taking down the ad.[14] Similarly, in Florida, gubernatorial candidate Charlie Crist violated school district rules when he filmed an ad at his former high school.[15] In Wisconsin, an ad that pictured Governor Scott Walker climbing up a ladder led a union leader to file a complaint with the Occupational Health and Safety Administration about the unsafe working conditions during filming.[16]

Recently, candidates' campaigns have found a way to help groups that air ads on their behalf by posting high-definition **B-roll video** of the candidates on their websites. This allows groups to use that footage of the candidate in their ads without violating bans on coordination between candidates and groups. Senator Mitch McConnell's posting of this type of B-roll was intensely ridiculed by Jon Stewart on *The Daily Show* when he devoted multiple episodes to setting the B-roll to various types of music, which he called "McConnelling," and encouraged viewers to create their own "McConnelling" videos and post them to social media.[17]

Ad Testing

Once the ad is created, it is often tested. This is especially likely to occur for presidential campaigns or campaigns in highly competitive Senate races, which have considerable financial resources. One way to test ads is with additional focus groups. Focus groups can identify which of multiple versions of an ad is most effective and can help identify when an ad's argument is confusing. If a focus group reacts negatively to a particular ad, it may be modified or even scrapped.

Campaigns may also conduct **dial testing**, in which anonymous participants move a dial in one direction or another while viewing the ad to register how much they like the ad at any point in time. Dial testing is particularly useful for measuring people's emotional responses to an ad and can help identify particular segments of the ad—maybe just a few seconds—that are particularly ineffective or counterproductive so that they can be modified.

More recently, campaigns have turned to online ad testing. Companies that specialize in this type of research typically ask a fairly large sample of individuals to view an ad online and then answer questions—such as whether they find it believable, interesting, or informative—that are designed to measure its effectiveness. This allows the campaign to compare not just which ads are more effective but also which ads are most effective among particular groups of voters, such as political independents, men, or Latinos. The advantage of online ad testing over traditional focus groups is twofold: (1) campaigns can more quickly and easily reach a wide range of individuals to get their thoughts on a particular ad, and (2) citizens are reached in the comfort of their own homes, which is more akin to the way in which they encounter advertising in the real world and where they're unlikely to be influenced by others in the focus group.

As mentioned earlier in the chapter, online ad testing company Ace Metrix asked five hundred people to evaluate more than three hundred ads aired during the 2012 presidential campaign, including both television and online ads and ads sponsored by candidates, parties, and interest groups. Unlike most ad testing companies, Ace Metrix tested all presidential ads—both those favorable to Romney and those favorable to Obama—enabling comparisons across the full universe of presidential ads. Panelists were asked the degree to which they agreed that (1) they learned something from the ad, (2) the ad got their attention, (3) the ad was credible, (4) they would seek out more information on the ad's topic, (5) they personally connected with the ad, and (5) they agreed with the ad. They also were asked how likely they were to watch the ad again under certain circumstances. All of these measures were combined to create a measure of the ad's effectiveness.

While the "Stage" ad, as noted earlier, scored as highly effective, others did not fare as well. One ad that scored extremely low on the effectiveness scale was an online ad aired by Restore Our Future, a super PAC supporting Mitt Romney. The ad focused on a comment from a Democratic campaign strategist, Hillary Rosen, about Ann Romney's having never "worked a day in her life." It also focused on a comment made by comedian Bill Maher, an Obama supporter, who said that Ann Romney "has never gotten her ass out of the house." The ad ended with the female narrator saying, "Happy Mother's Day from Barack Obama's team."[18] This attack ad was not liked by participants in the online panel, who rated it the third least effective ad of the season. Women rated it slightly less effective than did men. Among women, it was the second least effective ad; among men, it was the fifth least effective ad. One reason this ad was likely so ineffective is that it focused on repeating personal attacks, something most citizens dislike and find unacceptable in advertising (a topic to which we'll return in future chapters). Furthermore, the attacks were not directly attributable to Obama, which may have increased perceptions that the ad was unfairly placing blame.

The ad with the largest discrepancy in effectiveness ratings between men and women panelists was one from the Obama campaign called "First Law." This ad was clearly designed to reach women voters: it featured a female narrator, contained images of Michelle Obama and the Obama daughters along with other mothers and daughters throughout, and focused on Obama's support for the Lilly Ledbetter Fair Pay Act, which was aimed at reducing the pay gap between men and women. The ad scored highly among women, but it ranked just 226 out of 366 ads tested among men. As we will discuss more extensively in future chapters, tailoring advertising messages to a particular audience may increase its effectiveness among the intended audience (in this case women),[19] but mistargeted voters (in this case men) may dislike and penalize the sponsor for the mistargeting.[20]

Final Production and Launch

Once ad testing is completed, final production of the ad takes place. Sometimes the content of the ad changes slightly as a result of focus group testing, and the language may be modified slightly because of lawyers' concerns about whether an attack opens up the campaign to a lawsuit. The voiceover, lighting, and transitions are also finalized to create a finished product that is sent on to television stations and posted on the sponsor's website.

The last step is launching the ad—an essential part of the process today. Campaigns and groups do not just start airing ads; they announce at press conferences and via social media that they are going to start airing a new ad. They post the ads to their websites and to YouTube. And they encourage reporters to write about their ads. All this is done in the hope of attracting free coverage from the news media—and free repetition of the claims made in the ad. Often the publicity around an ad is accompanied by (exaggerated) claims about how much the sponsor is spending to air the ad, which makes the campaign look more formidable. Research shows that, ultimately, campaign ads receive considerable free media coverage, something that we will discuss more in later chapters.

THE INTERNET, SOCIAL MEDIA, AND ADVERTISING

Although billions of dollars are still spent each year on televised political advertising, there is no doubt that advertising dollars are moving to online venues, though perhaps more slowly than one might expect given that online advertising is less expensive to purchase. Estimates vary, but it is safe to say that online advertising still constitutes a relatively small share of campaign ad budgets. That being said, it is worth considering how the move of advertising to the Internet might influence ad content.

One possibility is that online advertising could result in more creative ads, as ad makers are unconstrained by thirty-second time limits and requirements that they authorize their ads. Indeed, online ads that were posted in the 2012 campaign ranged from sixteen seconds to well over ten minutes. Linked to this is the possibility that ads with nontraditional sponsors, even everyday citizens, have a greater chance of becoming part of the political discourse. This could also result in more creative advertisements—perhaps ones that employ humor, which is rare in television advertising—and new formats, such as extremely short or long ads. Ad makers would be able to go beyond "the way it has always been done" in the creation of advertising. In the summer of 2007, for example, the humor website Barely Political (now Barely Productions) posted a three-minute-long video featuring "Obama girl," who sang about her crush on Obama. It has been viewed over twenty-six million times. Still, although the potential exists for nontraditional actors to be heard, many of the ads that go viral, whether designed for the web or not, are ones produced by the campaigns themselves or by more traditional outside groups.

Some report that the purpose of online advertising is somewhat different than that of traditional television advertising, which is, by and large, focused on persuasion or bringing partisans home. Online advertising, by contrast, seems to serve many more goals, including raising money and identifying and rallying supporters. These differences in purpose are likely driven by differences in audience. Many online ads are seen primarily by existing supporters of a candidate. Think about it: if you receive an e-mail that contains political information—perhaps a link to a political video that the sender would like you to view—it is much more likely to come from a friend who shares your politics or the campaign whose website you entered your e-mail address on than from someone on the other side of the political spectrum. Thus, candidates generally use their online ads not for persuasion but to encourage supporters to get out to vote, to contribute money, or to volunteer for the campaign.

Indeed, online advertisements sometimes target much smaller groups than television ads. Certainly, some television ads are designed to speak to specific groups and their concerns, such as women, immigrants, or working-class families. And presidential campaigns typically air Spanish-language ads on Univision or Telemundo in order to target Latino voters. But online ads can be even more effective at speaking to smaller demographic groups. The Obama campaign in 2012, for instance, posted a two-and-a-half-minute-long ad on its website that featured various people of Asian and Pacific Islander descent discussing what Obama had done for members of that community.[21] Another Obama ad posted online—this one seven minutes long and aimed at Jewish voters—spoke of Obama's effort to improve US ties with Israel and featured Ehud Barak, Israel's defense minister at the time, speaking in flattering terms about Obama.[22] Romney's website in 2012 had ads aimed at voters in individual states.

Online advertising also serves as an inexpensive and quick way to shape the news media's narrative. Posting an online ad that makes an outrageous, egregious attack against an opponent is a good way to get the news media to repeat that attack. Even if reporters point out that the attack is unfair, inaccurate, or only partially true, it still gets the specific charge out into the mind of the public. We will return to discussion of online advertising in Chapter 6.

CONCLUSION

Most political ads are carefully crafted. When designing ads, their makers carefully consider several elements of the ad's content, including its length, tone, visual imagery, voiceover and music, and the approval line. All of these elements of an ad combine to create a particular mood that can help to convey the ad's central message and make the ad more effective. Ad testing helps ad makers know how and when to refine these elements of an ad by providing them with the opinions of many individuals through focus groups, dial groups, or online surveys.

Ad creation, testing, and refinement are nothing new, but they have become much more sophisticated with the development of new technologies. As campaigns are able to target smaller and smaller groups (both in more targeted television buys, which we'll discuss in Chapter 5, and in online advertising, which we'll discuss at length in Chapter 6), advertising content is increasingly tailored to smaller subgroups of the public. On the one hand, this tailoring makes it more likely that campaigns discuss precisely the issues the targeted population cares about. On the other hand, as we noted in Chapter 1, it may make campaigns increasingly about "nothing" as the campaign experience may differ from person to person. We'll discuss the consequences and risks of targeting and tailoring in Chapter 7.

DISCUSSION QUESTIONS

1. Why do campaigns care so much about the components of an ad? Do you think that small things like color and music matter? Why or why not?
2. Put yourself in the role of campaign manager. Would you want to tailor your campaign's messages to be slightly different for different audiences? Why or why not?
3. As a citizen, how comfortable are you knowing that campaigns tailor their advertising to different audiences? Explain.
4. Which do you believe would be more effective: a fifteen-second ad or a sixty-second ad? Why?

NOTES

1. https://www.youtube.com/watch?v=QxVqi8fuPDs.

2. University of Wisconsin Advertising Project, Historic Ads Archive, http://wiscadproject.wisc.edu/history.php.

3. David Weigel, "From Their Cold, Dead Hands," *Slate*, May 9, 2014, http://www.slate.com/articles/news_and_politics/politics/2014/05/republicans

_shooting_guns_gop_candidates_are_advertising_how_they_fire_a.html; Don Gonyea, "Guns Boom in 2014 Campaign Ads," *All Things Considered,* NPR, September, 1, 2014, http://www.npr.org/2014/09/01/344339046/guns-boom-in-2014 -campaign-ads.

4. Darrell M. West, *Air Wars: Television Advertising and Social Media in Election Campaigns, 1952–2012* (Los Angeles: Sage, 2013).

5. Patricia Strach, Katherine Zuber, Erika Franklin Fowler, Travis N. Ridout, and Kathleen Searles, "In a Different Voice? Explaining the Use of Men and Women as Voice-Over Announcers in Political Advertising," *Political Communication* 32, no. 2 (2015): 183–205.

6. Michael M. Franz, Joel Rivlin, and Kenneth Goldstein, "Much More of the Same: Television Advertising Pre- and Post-BCRA," in *The Election After Reform: Money, Politics, and the Bipartisan Campaign Reform Act*, ed. Michael J. Malbin (Lanham, MD: Rowman and Littlefield, 2006), 139–162.

7. Jordyn Phelps, "'Hardheaded' Sen. Mary Landrieu and Dad Team Up for Cute Campaign Ad," *ABC News,* May 13, 2014, http://abcnews.go.com/blogs /politics/2014/05/hardheaded-sen-mary-landrieu-and-dad-team-up-for-cute -campaign-ad.

8. D. W. Johnson, *No Place for Amateurs: How Political Consultants Are Reshaping American Democracy,* 2nd ed. (New York: Routledge, 2007).

9. Jeremy W. Peters, "The New Stars in Republican Commercials Attacking Obama: Babies," *New York Times,* September 29, 2012, http://www.nytimes.com /2012/09/30/us/politics/gop-strategists-ads-warn-president-obama-is-bad-for -babies.html.

10. Jeremy W. Peters, "'Dear Daughter,'" The Caucus, *New York Times,* September 19, 2012, http://thecaucus.blogs.nytimes.com/2012/09/19/dear-daughter.

11. https://www.youtube.com/watch?v=IKYcMZFhzcc.

12. Jeremy W. Peters, "The Selling of a Politician, and the Ads Almost Broadcast," *New York Times,* March 22, 2012, http://www.nytimes.com/2012/03/23/us /politics/the-selling-of-a-politician-and-the-ads-almost-broadcast.html.

13. https://www.youtube.com/watch?v=THuHoC6SVpk.

14. Amanda Terkel, "GOP Congressman Violated Rules by Filming Campaign Ad at Veterans Cemetery," *Huffington Post,* October 6, 2014, http://www .huffingtonpost.com/2014/10/06/kevin-cramer-veterans_n_5940942.html.

15. Cara Fitzpatrick, "Crist Ad Violates Pinellas County School District's Rules," *Tampa Bay Times,* July 30, 2014, http://www.tampabay.com/news/education/crist -political-ad-shot-at-st-petersburg-high-violated-school-district/2190733.

16. Meredith Clark, "Union Head Files OSHA Complaint over Scott Walker Ad," *MSNBC,* September 17, 2014, http://www.msnbc.com/msnbc/union-head -files-osha-complaint-over-scott-walker-ad.

17. Jaime Fuller, "How 'McConnelling' Came to Be the Hottest Thing on the Political Web," The Fix (blog), *Washington Post,* March 14, 2014, http://www

.washingtonpost.com/blogs/the-fix/wp/2014/03/14/how-mcconnelling-came-to
-be/.

18. https://www.youtube.com/watch?v=mV6Dn8qMzig.

19. Patricia Strach, Katherine Zuber, Erika Franklin Fowler, Travis N. Ridout, and Kathleen Searles, "In a Different Voice? Explaining the Use of Men and
Women as Voice-Over Announcers in Political Advertising," *Political Communication* 32, no. 2 (2015): 183–205.

20. Eitan D. Hersh and Brian F. Schaffner, "Targeted Campaign Appeals and
the Value of Ambiguity," *Journal of Politics* 75, no. 2 (2013): 520–534.

21. https://www.youtube.com/watch?v=PPjNd5l9FzE.

22. https://www.youtube.com/watch?v=izUkZpTft2w.

CHAPTER 5

Buying and Targeting Political Advertising on Television

Having discussed how political ads are created and tested, we turn our attention to the buying and targeting of televised political advertising; that is, how ad sponsors determine where an ad should be placed so it can best reach its target audience. In races for the US Senate in 2014, 980,594 ads aired on local broadcast stations between January 1 and Election Day. And ad sponsors in 2014—up and down the ballot—placed ads on over fifteen thousand unique programs. Tracking when political ads aired and on what networks and shows is as important as analyzing the content and sponsorship of ads in measuring the impact of political advertising.

In this chapter, we begin by discussing the variety of decisions that go into buying advertising time on television. Next, we look at the different types of networks on which ad sponsors might choose to air their ads, and we examine the targeting of ads to programs or television genres that feature different audience profiles. We look at how the changing media landscape has affected the targeting of political advertising and analyze the relationships between ad airings and media consumption to illuminate the trends and future of targeted political advertising. A key conclusion that we draw from this analysis is that ad targeting is upending the way voters see ads, but we are only in the early stages of this change. More change is on the way and will be evident in ad patterns in future campaigns.

BUYING DECISIONS

Most campaigns outsource the actual purchase of television airtime to media buyers, who typically work on commission. This commission can be up to 15 percent, so if the buyer contracts with a television station to air twenty thousand dollars' worth of ads, he or she could earn three thousand dollars. Thus, there is an incentive for media buyers to encourage campaigns to buy more advertising: the more advertising they place, the more money they make.

One decision that buyers help campaigns make is how much airtime to purchase for each unique ad, for different weeks of the campaign. Typically, media buyers do not think in terms of number of airings but in terms of **gross ratings points (GRPs)**. GRPs measure the reach of an advertising campaign; one GRP is equal to 1 percent of the potential targeted audience. So if 10 percent of the target audience, such as men younger than age thirty-five, have their televisions tuned to a station during a period in which your ad airs three times, you would have thirty (ten times three) GRPs. One old rule of thumb is that an ad should receive one thousand GRPs. At that point, the average viewer will have seen it ten times, so its effectiveness may begin to diminish with further viewings. This does not mean, however, that all viewers have in actuality seen the ad ten times; some may have seen it twenty times, while others may not have seen it at all. Thus, GRPs do not tell the full story of an ad's actual reach.

The cost of airing an ad varies considerably depending on the size of the audience, the desirability of the audience, and competition for airtime. Larger audiences mean greater impact, so it is more expensive to place an ad on programs with big audiences. Audience size depends first on the size of the media market. For instance, Senate candidate Dick Durbin paid $7,600 for an ad aired in September 2014 during the local ten o'clock news in Chicago, one of the largest media markets in the country. But Durbin paid only $800 to air an ad at the same time in the Champaign-Springfield-Decatur, Illinois, media market, which is the ninety-fifth largest media market in the country. Audience size depends also on the popularity of the program. On November 3, 2014, in Des Moines, Iowa, some advertisers paid over two thousand dollars to air a single ad on the highly ranked *Channel 8 News* at ten o'clock. But it cost only sixty dollars to place an ad at the same time in Des Moines on *Celebrity Name Game,* a program with a much smaller audience. The time of the day—known as **daypart** in the business—also affects audience size. Typically, the largest audiences are found watching television during **prime time**, which is eight to eleven p.m. in the Eastern and Pacific time zones and seven to ten p.m. in the Central and Mountain time zones.

The desirability of an audience also has an impact on how much airtime costs. A campaign's ad has more potential impact if it's shown to a group of citizens important to the campaign. For example, programs that attract swing voters who are highly likely to turn out to vote, like the local news, are very desirable. Programs that attract younger viewers who are unlikely to turn out to vote, like *The Vampire Diaries* or *The Voice,* are less desirable and thus charge less for airtime.

Finally, there is more competition for airtime in some media markets and at some points of the campaign. In 2014, Denver saw an onslaught of political advertising due to well-funded, competitive races for governor and US senator and representative. With many candidates and campaigns wanting airtime, television stations can and do raise their rates. Typically, there is much more competition for airtime the closer it is to Election Day, which increases the cost of purchasing airtime then, too. The average political ad in October 2014 cost about $670, compared to about $425 in March. (We covered some of this in Chapter 2.)

Another decision that campaigns must make in conjunction with media buyers is when to buy airtime. Lately, the preferred strategy has been to lock in airtime early. This not only allows campaigns to secure cheaper rates, it also ensures that they have airtime booked in October, when there may be intense competition from candidates and groups. Campaigns do not want to run the risk of being off the air because airtime is too expensive. What's more, locking in airtime early can telegraph to one's allies what the campaign's advertising strategy is. For instance, if an independent group locks in airtime in a particular media market for October, it sends a signal to the favored candidate's campaign—with which it is not legally allowed to coordinate—to place its advertising elsewhere. Of course, one downside is that locking in advertising early can also tip off an opponent to one's strategy.

ADVERTISING ON DIFFERENT TELEVISION NETWORKS

The default choice for advertising on television is local broadcast networks. Yet the media markets served by local broadcast television stations and congressional districts seldom line up well. Take, for instance, Alabama's third congressional district, which covers eastern central Alabama (see Figure 5.1). About 47 percent of the district's residents live in the Birmingham media market.[1] Another third of the district's residents live in the Columbus, Georgia, media market. About 14 percent live in the Montgomery, Alabama, media market, and another 5 percent live in the Atlanta, Georgia, media market. Voters in the district may share a member of Congress, but they are watching television stations based in four different major cities. Candidates for Alabama's third congressional district seat must therefore buy advertising on television stations in four different markets in order to speak to all of the district's voters, a very expensive proposition. Not only that, but much of the money will be wasted. Most of the people living in the Atlanta media market do not care about Alabama's third district because they vote in other districts. And yet ad sponsors pay extremely high rates to buy ads in the ninth-largest media market in the country.[2]

These inefficiencies caused by the mismatch between the borders of congressional districts and media markets are not just present in US House races. In races for the Senate, there are inefficiencies when media markets cross state boundaries, as they do in places like St. Louis, Philadelphia, and Washington, DC, which covers parts of four states. In

Figure 5.1: Alabama's Third Congressional District and Media Market Overlap

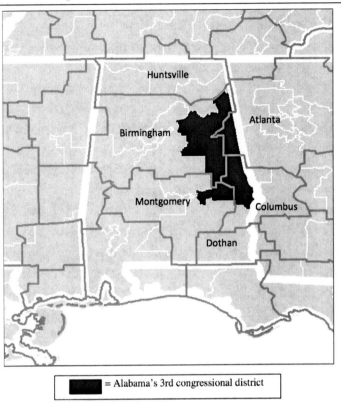

= Alabama's 3rd congressional district

Source: Laura Baum, Wesleyan Media Project

presidential races, ad sponsors want to focus mostly on reaching voters in swing states, and even more specifically swing media markets in swing states. They might run ads in Boston in order to reach voters in New Hampshire, a battleground state, but they are still wasting money in speaking to those solidly blue voters in Massachusetts who have voted for the Democratic Party nominee in every election since 1988. And, of course, the problem may be even worse for those running for an office that covers an even smaller geographic area, such as county commissioner, city council member, or state representative.

Given the inefficiencies associated with airing political ads on broadcast television, it seems reasonable that candidates and other ad sponsors would pursue other avenues. Some certainly do, avoiding television entirely and using more traditional means of communication, such as mailers, radio ads, or even billboards, in addition to the online advertising that we will discuss in Chapter 6. But it is rare for a candidate to avoid television advertising entirely if he or she is running in a competitive race for Congress, let alone running for governor, senator, or president, because television advertising reaches larger audiences and is more effective in persuading voters. In spite of the inefficiencies, local broadcast television remains the primary way for political ad sponsors to get out their messages.

Campaigns are not limited to local broadcast television, however; there are other options. A **national broadcast television** ad is one that airs to all Americans during network shows, like *Survivor* on CBS or *Saturday Night Live* on NBC. Buying an ad on national broadcast television is extremely expensive because it is aired across the country, not just in one small geographic area. The only situation in which buying such ads might make sense is in a presidential race, where candidates are seeking votes across the country, but even then it may be inefficient because candidates are primarily concerned with winning the dozen or so competitive battleground states. Nonetheless, the Obama campaign did air a few ads on national broadcast television during his 2012 reelection campaign, as did Restore Our Future, a super PAC created to support Mitt Romney.

Why would presidential campaigns air ads on national broadcast television? One reason is that it may help to raise the candidate's percentage of the popular vote nationally. Second, close to Election Day, when the cost of advertising on local broadcast television in swing states shoots up due to competition for airtime, it may actually be cheaper to buy a national ad than to pay the inflated prices in all of the battleground media markets. Third, if the ad inspires the candidate's supporters to show up to vote, that may help candidates of the same party lower on the ballot.

Another option for presidential candidates is to air advertising on **national cable networks,** such as HGTV, ESPN, or Lifetime. Advertising on national cable television has some of the same inefficiencies as national broadcast television, and thus it is only used by presidential candidates—particularly those seeking the party nomination, who may find the segmentation of audiences on different cable channels appealing. Those running for the Republican Party's presidential nomination are likely to run an ad on Fox News because much of its audience consists of politically active Republicans who are highly likely to vote in a primary or caucus—and, in fact, in the 2012 presidential primary season, super PACs backing Newt Gingrich and Mitt Romney aired ads on Fox News. Similarly, Democratic primary candidates are likely to run ads on MSNBC because its audience consists primarily of politically active Democrats. In the general election in 2012, however, CNN was the most popular cable news channel for advertising, in part because its audiences includes both Democrats and Republicans (whereas FOX and MSNBC have more partisan audiences), attracting more than eight hundred ad buys from the Obama campaign and more than three hundred ad buys from the Republican Party. Yet campaigns did not only stick to news networks. In fact, the Travel Channel saw more ads in the general election presidential campaign than any other cable network, in part because campaigns need to reach voters who may not pay a lot of attention to politics but can be persuaded to turn out to support a candidate.

One other venue in which candidates and other sponsors air ads is **local cable television.** Between programs airing on national cable networks, cable companies are able to run some ads that are seen only in particular cities or even neighborhoods. These geographic areas, called *zones,* are smaller than media markets. For instance, roughly five zones cover the city of Chicago. A candidate for mayor of Chicago can pay to air ads in just those five zones. An ad on local broadcast television, by contrast, would also reach voters in the suburbs and parts of Indiana and Wisconsin as well. Thus, airing ads on local cable, which tend to reach only those individuals eligible to vote in a particular race, can be much more efficient than airing them on broadcast television.

You might think, then, that political candidates would be rushing to put their money into local cable, and to a point they are. It's estimated that sixty-two million dollars was spent on political advertising on local cable television in the 2012 presidential race,[3] and one estimate puts local cable spending in 2014 at 25 percent of total ad spending.[4] One reason for the growth is that the cable industry has made it easier for ad sponsors to buy time. They have developed **cable interconnects** that allow an ad sponsor to make a single purchase that spans multiple cable systems, so instead of dealing with several different cable companies to get their ads placed, they can deal with just one seller—NCC Media, a company that was organized by the cable industry to handle cable television ad purchases. In addition, campaigns and campaign consultants are getting better at data analytics and targeting, which means they now are able to tell which very specific types of voters— much more specific than "women ages eighteen to thirty-four" or "men older than sixty-five"—are watching particular cable networks and programs, making it more appealing to buy airtime on local cable to reach desirable groups. We will discuss how this targeting is done in more depth later in the chapter.

There are some things holding back the growth of political advertising on local cable television, however. One is a limited supply of airtime. Most of the time is allotted to national advertisers, like car companies, that want everyone on national cable to see their ads, leaving very little time for ads that are only seen locally. Thus, even though political campaigns may want to use local cable more frequently, they are often unable to purchase airtime, especially when there are multiple competitive races on the ballot. A second factor is that it is difficult to reach large audiences by airing a few ads on several cable channels. The size of the audience for any one cable network is small compared the size of the audience watching a local broadcast channel. So if a campaign wants to get out a message to a lot of voters quickly (or to the news media in order to set a narrative), local cable television may be a poor way to do so.

Although there are no comprehensive data on the cost and airings of local cable ads as there is for broadcast advertising, there are some scattered data about campaigns' use of local cable. For instance, one of the big cable television companies, Time Warner, posts its public file online. From that we can see that in late June of 2014, Senate candidate Kay Hagan paid just five dollars per ad for airtime on the Hallmark Channel in Elizabeth City, North Carolina, a town of about twenty thousand people. Undoubtedly, very few people in Elizabeth City saw that ad, but the price was hard to beat. In much larger Greensboro, by contrast, the Hagan campaign paid $200 per ad for airtime on USA Network during prime time and paid $156 per ad on TNT.

The 2012 presidential race gives us an opportunity to compare the percentage of campaign advertising that goes to each kind of television distribution. Of the little more than one billion dollars spent on advertising in the 2012 presidential race, it is estimated that 87.5 percent was spent on local broadcast advertising, 6.1 percent on local cable, 2.9 percent on national cable, and 3.5 percent on national network advertising.[5] In terms of dollar amounts, then, local broadcast television still dominates. But it is important to keep in mind a couple of things. First, candidates in down-ballot races do not use national advertising, but they are probably more likely to use local cable advertising than presidential candidates, given that local candidates want to speak to a more geographically constrained area. Second, although local cable spending may be a fairly small share of advertising spending, that spending buys a lot of ad airings when you're only paying five or eight dollars apiece.

TARGETING POLITICAL ADVERTISING

Now that we have discussed the different types of television distribution and the reasoning behind where sponsors choose to place their ads, let us delve deeper and explore trends in **ad targeting**, which is the practice of strategically placing ads on programs whose viewers belong to the demographic groups that sponsors want to reach. Consider, for example, the Senate campaign in Louisiana in 2014. Democratic incumbent Mary Landrieu—who went on to lose the election in a December runoff—aired nearly thirty thousand ads on local broadcast stations that year. She placed these ads on a range of programs, including popular syndicated court shows like *Judge Judy* and *Judge Mathis*. Landrieu and her party and interest group allies aired 2,989 ads on those two court shows plus a few others (such as the *People's Court*), compared to just 748 spots from Republican Bill Cassidy and his allies. This isn't surprising, considering data on audience composition compiled by Scarborough Research, which polls hundreds of thousands of Americans each year on their consumer and media habits. In their 2010 polling on about twenty genres of television shows, from sports to religious programs, court shows were the genre most disproportionately Democratic in terms of viewers.[6] Clearly, by concentrating ads on court shows, Landrieu and her allies were trying to speak to Democratic voters—those most likely to respond to, and be motivated by, her message.

However, one conclusion we draw in our exploration of the ad data is that targeting is still fairly new, and television ads don't always dramatically skew in a predictable direction. The same polling that found that viewers of court shows are overwhelmingly Democratic also found that viewers of sporting events skew Republican. But in the same Louisiana race, Cassidy and his allies placed just 490 spots during sports programming (a low number given that they placed half again as many spots during court shows), while Landrieu and her allies aired a fairly comparable 435 spots. More generally in 2014, Democrats and Republicans aired roughly the same number of total ads across all shows, but there was a slight imbalance in sports programming. In House races, Democrats aired 44 percent of the ads during sports programming, and in Senate races, Democrats were responsible for 40 percent of the ads. This is certainly in line with expectations, but it might be surprising that Democrats put so many ads on such shows.[7] Therefore, while ad targeting represents a new means for campaigns to speak to particular groups of voters and be more directed in their outreach efforts, we have not yet reached a point where ads simply reinforce and reproduce partisan polarization. In other words, while

Democratic campaigns may be more likely to target Democrats, a lot of Republicans are still being exposed to Democratic ads, and a lot of Democrats are exposed to Republican ads.

Indeed, political practitioners note that the sophisticated targeting of political ads is a fairly recent phenomenon. According to media buyer Will Feltus, there are four generations of ad targeting. The first began in the 1960s, when ad-buying strategies were relatively blunt. Campaigns targeted broad demographic groups by purchasing spots in certain times of days (for example, daytime for female voters, prime time for a mix of women and men). The second generation began only in 2004. This iteration used survey data to account for the viewer profiles of different television programs. For instance, surveys revealed which programs were watched by Democrats, which by Republicans, and which by people who were likely to vote. Since 2012, a third generation of targeting has emerged wherein campaigns learn about viewing habits not only from detailed surveys but also from people's cable boxes and satellite dishes. These devices can collect very detailed data on what we watch and thus have become another way for campaigns to learn which *types* of voters are watching which types of programs.[8] The fourth generation of targeting, which involves the use of individually **addressable ads,** has been tried on a small scale with satellite television subscribers but is poised to take off in the 2016 campaigns. Here ads are targeted to specific households, not just specific programs. Thus, subscribers to satellite television can be shown ads that vary from household to household—even on the same block.

In addition to the availability of more detailed viewer data, the recent proliferation of specialized cable programs and online streaming channels has also made ad targeting more sophisticated. Although niche programming draws in a smaller audience, that audience tends to be more uniform, which means that ad sponsors can find audiences that fit very specific profiles across the television dial (or cable box) and direct their advertising accordingly. For example, to appeal to younger Democrats, a candidate might advertise on Comedy Central's *Inside Amy Schumer*. To appeal to older Republicans, he or she might advertise on the History Channel's *Pawn Stars*. This is part of a larger trend in American elections towards **microtargeting**, in which campaigns use available public and private data both to locate partisans for get-out-the-vote messages and to reach specific independents or opposing partisans for persuasion messages.[9]

THE CHANGING MEDIA LANDSCAPE AND ITS EFFECT ON VOTERS

The changing media landscape has had powerful effects on the way campaigns reach voters on television. Put simply, how people watch television is very different today than it was twenty or thirty years ago. Nielsen has reported regularly on the audience profile of prime time viewers. In 1985, 45 percent of all US households tuned in to watch the three broadcast networks—ABC, NBC, and CBS—and their local affiliates.[10] Nearly 70 percent of television viewers in 1985 were watching shows on the "Big Three" networks at any point between seven p.m. and eleven p.m. By 2009, only 25 percent of US households were watching networks,[11] which amounted to only 34 percent of those watching television during prime time on a typical night. In just twenty-five years the **network affiliates**—local television stations that broadcast the networks' programs—have seen their audience share cut in half. This stark decline is even more pronounced when one considers that Nielsen now includes in its viewership totals anyone who watches shows on network affiliates within seven days of their original airing (through DVR or on-demand). This decline can be attributed to the proliferation of cable channels and alternative viewing options. Citizens today have many more choices when they turn on the television, which means smaller and more fragmented audiences for most programs.

Moreover, the media landscape is still changing. A small but not trivial number of Americans are **cutting the cord**, a term that refers to dropping cable or satellite television service in favor of streaming video via an Internet connection to a computer, tablet, or television set. In 2014, 7.3 percent of households had cut the cord, up from 4.2 percent in 2010.[12] These households are likely to stream video from their tablet or phone to their television or use an Internet TV device like Roku or Apple TV. And while cord-cutters are watching many network or cable programs (through services like Hulu, Amazon Prime, and Netflix), the ads on streaming video—unlike on traditional television—can be tailored to specific viewers or households. (We say more about online ads and ad targeting online in Chapter 6.)

Political scientists have documented these trends in recent years and have largely lamented their effects on voters. For example, Markus Prior notes that with the development and spread of cable television, viewers who prefer entertainment over news can largely opt out of all political news on television.[13] That is, for those who are interested primarily in reality television and sitcoms and who want to hear very little about current affairs, politics, the economy, international finance, or US military interventions, there are a number of channels that deliver that preferred content, and nothing but that content. This has resulted in a **knowledge gap**, in which apolitical viewers know even less about politics (compared to the years when there were only three television stations) because they can easily avoid it, while those interested in politics learn even more as they flock to the cable channels that satisfy their appetites for such content. Increased choice in the media environment can also lead to more politically segmented viewership: Democrats and Republicans tend to self-select into watching news channels that support their worldviews.[14]

Although this knowledge gap may be disconcerting to some, for advocates of political advertising—such as the political consultants who make the ads and buy the airtime, along with the candidates, who hope to speak to likely voters—these changes represent an opportunity to speak directly to audiences of different types. As we illustrated earlier with the 2014 US Senate race in Louisiana, campaigns are already using this to their advantage. If polling suggests that sitcom and game show fans skew Democratic, then Republican campaigners can largely avoid those shows to save the lost money and time of trying to convince the opposition, while Democrats can target them.

However, changes in the distribution of television programming have not meant a decline in the amount of time spent watching television. Quite the contrary—Americans continue to consume a significant amount of television, and it remains their primary form of entertainment. Nielsen reported that the average US household watches about ninety minutes of television during prime time each night, and this number has not budged in the last twenty years.[15] What has changed is the total time spent watching television over the course of the day, which steadily *increased* from about four and a half hours in 1952 to seven hours in 1985 to nearly eight and a half hours in 2009.

In fact, television is still a primary means by which most Americans get their news. For example, Pew reported in 2012 that 55 percent of Americans get their news primarily from television (a largely stable number since the mid-1990s), followed by 39 percent online (up from 24 percent in 2002), 33 percent from a newspaper (and declining fast), and 29 percent from the radio (also waning, down from about 40 percent in 2002). Television's comparative advantage remains robust despite the growth of online news consumption (including on mobile devices) in recent years.[16] A different Pew study in 2013 reported that 71 percent of Americans had watched a local television news program in the previous month, while 65 percent had watched a national network news program.[17] Of course, many people get information from multiple platforms, and they often do it simultaneously, surfing the web or reading on a tablet while also watching their favorite television program. Still, television clearly remains a focal point for Americans.

EXAMINING AD TARGETING THROUGH AD AIRINGS AND MEDIA CONSUMPTION DATA

In this section, we'll take what we now know about Americans' media consumption habits and combine it with the Wesleyan Media Project's rich data on ad airings to examine a couple of key issues concerning ad targeting. First, even with the variety of programming available today, sponsors still overwhelmingly favor placing their ads on news shows. Given that, are there relationships between the data on ad airings and the data on media habits that point to evidence of ad targeting? How have some of these relationships changed over time, and how do they vary across sponsors or races?

But first, a note on the data: although the data encompass national and local broadcast buys as well as national cable, it is important to note that there are limitations to the picture it presents because we do not have information about local cable buys. There is evidence to suggest that such local cable buys are still relatively small in terms of total ad spending, but their numbers are large and growing. For example, one report in October 2013 demonstrated that $340 million was spent on local cable ad buys in 2008. That number grew to $445 million in 2010 and $625 million in 2012. The expectation was that 2014 would exceed $700 million.[18] That is a lot of money, doubling between 2008 and 2014, but it still represented only 25 percent of the expected ad spending in 2014. Local broadcast is still the much bigger game in town.

Still, ad targeting is likely *underestimated*, since the ad data cover programs with the broadest audience profiles. As one might imagine, niche programs on cable channels are the real place to look for viewers of specific stripes. Indeed, the media have reported many times on the different shows popular among Democrats and Republicans. As one headline reported, "Republicans Like Golf, Democrats Prefer Cartoons." The article stated that "television viewing . . . is every bit as polarized as the political culture,"[19] but we are limited in what we can show in this chapter given the lack of local cable data on where and when campaigns and other ad sponsors buy political ads.

Majority of Ads Air on News Programming

One fact stands out in our analysis of ad buys by program and show genres: a majority of ads air on news shows, and that has been true for the last decade and a half. Figure 5.2 shows the percentage of ads aired on news broadcasts in congressional and gubernatorial races between 2000 and 2014, and for presidential races between 2000 and 2012. We also show the percentage of ads aired on game shows and talk shows— the next most frequent placement for political ads.[20]

A fair estimate is that about 60 percent of local broadcast ads in the covered races, across all years, air on news shows. Some slight change is evident in the graph, though it should not be overstated. For example, the placement of ads on news programs has trended down in presidential elections, quite noticeably between 2000 and 2008. The slight decline is likely the result of more-sophisticated targeting decisions by presidential campaigns,[21] while the uptick in 2012 is probably a consequence of more traditional ad buying by varying sponsors in that race.

On the whole, the percentage of ads purchased by congressional and gubernatorial campaigns on news programs has stayed remarkably consistent across time. Why such consistency, especially in light of the discussion so far in this chapter? One reason is the ubiquity of news programming. Many stations air two to three hours each day of locally produced newscasts, so there is simply more airtime available during news programs for campaigns to purchase.

Perhaps more importantly, though, is that the audience for local news remains an ideal target for political campaigns. Certainly, campaigns want to reach their core supporters and encourage them to participate. They also want to reach voters in the other party, especially if those voters are not as enthusiastic about their own party's candidate. But winning over voters in the other party is tough. More critical is appealing to swing voters and viewers who are likely to vote. A report in the *Washington Times* in September 2012 noted these issues with respect to television news:

> The people who watch news are those who still want to consume balanced information to help them make up their minds. While the plethora of cable networks has siphoned staunch Republicans to Fox News Channel for their national political news, and liberals go to MSNBC, *moderates have remained with traditional news programs* [our emphasis]. . . .
>
> The campaigns know a lot about the demographics of who's watching what. With younger Americans—who are much less likely

Figure 5.2: Percentage of Ads Aired During News Broadcasts Versus Game Shows and Talk Shows, 2000–2014

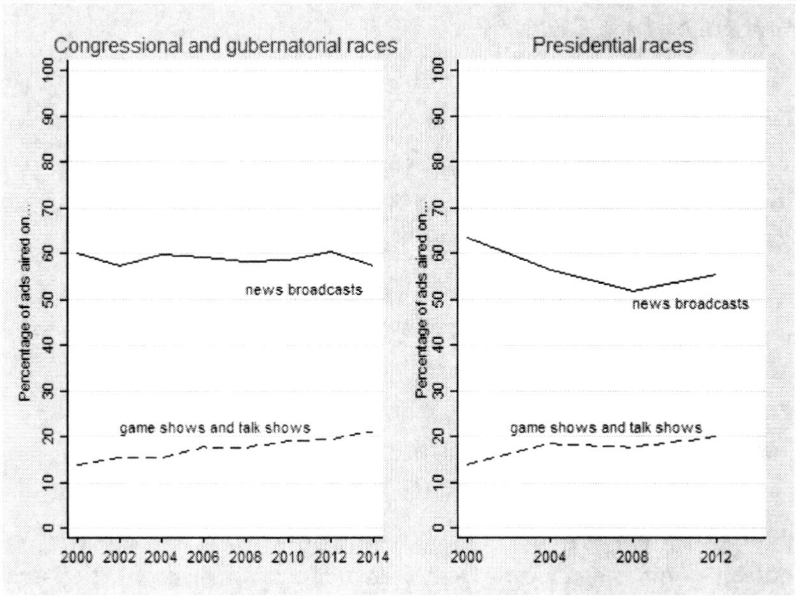

Includes all local broadcast ads in the election year. *Sources:* Raw data from Wisconsin Advertising Project and Wesleyan Media Project

to vote and also more likely to be committed Democrats—getting their news online, broadcast news is a straight path to older adults.[22]

Moreover, the Pew Research Center's biannual media consumption surveys consistently show that the partisan breakdown of local television news viewers, in contrast to the audiences of many cable news programs, most closely matches the partisan distribution of the country. Perhaps more importantly, local television news is the only source that draws a majority of both self-identified Republican and Democratic viewers and a near majority of independents.[23] In this sense, television news remains largely a place for broad outreach to voters.[24] In competitive elections, the margins matter the most. Campaigns need to win the majority of swing voters to have the best chance of winning the election. This is why news programming continues to be an appealing place to buy ads.

Evidence of Ad Targeting

However, the data do reveal some important evidence of ad targeting. First, we'll look at the distribution of ad buys by program genre in 2014. Second, we'll examine ad frequency over the course of the day for the presidential candidates in 2012 and Senate candidates in 2014. Finally, we'll dig into differences in targeting among ad sponsors for the presidential candidates and their allies in 2012.

Figure 5.3 shows the percentage of ads aired on behalf of Democrats in a wide range of program genres. Larger circles indicate program genres during which larger numbers of ads were shown.[25]

The results point to many partisan imbalances across program genres. Moreover, those imbalances make sense given what we know about the viewers of those shows. For example, we discussed at the outset of this chapter that Democrats tend to air disproportionately fewer ads than Republicans on all sports shows. When we disaggregate sports programs, we see that disparity more explicitly. Across all genres in House races, Democrats aired fewer ads in about thirty genres. Twenty-three of those genres were sports-related. Democrats out-advertised Republicans in only seven types of sports programming. For example, House Democrats sponsored about 60 percent of ads on tennis programs, while Republicans were responsible for nearly 80 percent of ads during college basketball games. We need to be cautious in stating these differences, though. As the figure makes clear, the programs with the most extreme overrepresentation by party featured incredibly small total ad buys, sometimes fewer than ten spots across all races. The program genres with the larger ad buys are clustered closer to the overall mean across ads in House and Senate contests.

Although Democrats bought a fair number of ads on news programming (represented by the largest bubble in each panel of Figure 5.3), it drew disproportionately more ads from Republicans. During local news in House races, 55 percent of ads aired were Republican-sponsored, and during local news in Senate races, 57 percent of ads

Figure 5.3: Program Genres and Percentage of Ads by Democrats in 2014

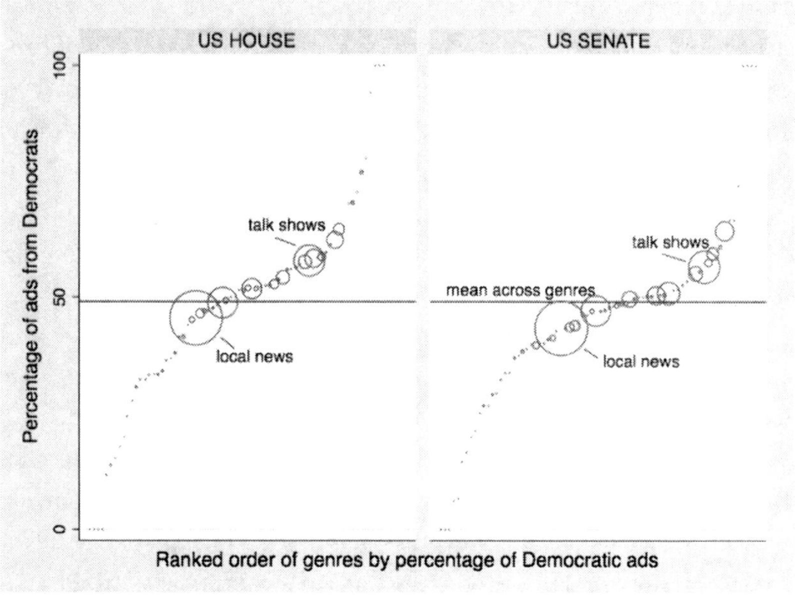

Circles scaled by total ads in genre. *Sources:* Raw data from Wisconsin Advertising Project and Wesleyan Media Project

aired were Republican-sponsored. We noted earlier that one appeal of local news is its diverse viewership, which allows campaigns to reach swing voters and base voters at the same time. Some research suggests, though, that Republicans are slightly more likely to report television as their *main* source of news. In a June 2013 Gallup poll, 63 percent of Republican respondents cited television as their main news source, compared to 54 percent of Democrats and 52 percent of independents.[26] This could account for the imbalance of ads from Republicans on local news. In contrast, Democrats in House and Senate races aired disproportionately more ads on drama and adventure programming, entertainment magazines, talk shows, sitcoms, and "slice-of-life" shows (including court shows and talent/reality competitions like *Dancing with the Stars* and *The Biggest Loser*). These all featured substantial numbers of spots and were often dominated by pro-Democratic ads.

Another fascinating finding about ad targeting is the disparity in the partisanship of ad sponsorship during different times of the day. For example, regular viewers at every point of the day—save for the prime time hours—are disproportionately Democrats.[27] Republicans are much less likely to watch television, with the exception of certain spikes in the early morning and a surge of television viewing during prime time. Indeed, prime time is the one time of the day where Democrats and Republicans watch television at roughly the same rate. Might these differences result in different patterns of ad buying for the two parties?

Figure 5.4 shows the frequency of ads shown over the course of an average day in the 2012 presidential election and all 2014 Senate elections. The graph plots the density of ads shown as a percentage of each party's total ads, so when the two lines are at the same height on the graph, it means that the two parties devoted the same *proportion* of their ads to that particular time slot, not the same *number* of ads.

The results suggest two interesting lessons. First, both parties advertise more heavily in the early evening and prime time hours, followed by late evening—around the time many watch their late local news—and early morning. Ad spots drop throughout the course of the day, bottoming out around two p.m. As one might imagine, there are almost no political ads in the middle of the night. These timing patterns make a lot of sense. The amount of television that Americans consume over the course of a day is actually quite stable. That is, if one splits the day into various parts—morning, daytime, prime time, and late night, Americans on average watch at least an hour of television in each part of the day, though the heaviest viewing is in prime time.[28] What is more important to political ad sponsors is the type of viewer watching television at various points throughout the day. Nielsen reported that Americans who make less than thirty thousand dollars a year devote 163 percent more minutes to watching television in the daytime than Americans who make more than one hundred thousand dollars a year. For those with only a high school diploma, the daytime viewing rate is double that of those with a college diploma. The income and education gap for all other parts of the day is less stark.

Figure 5.4: Ad Frequencies over the Course of a Day

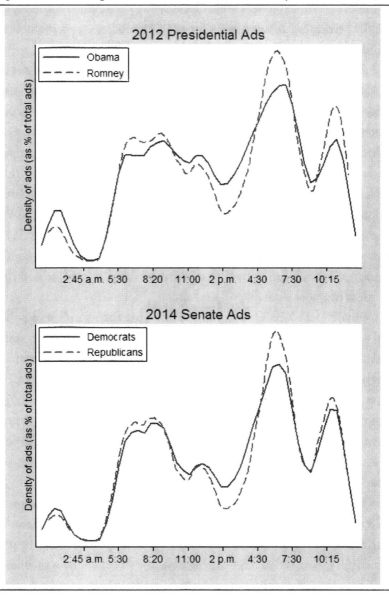

The plotted points show the average density of ads for certain times of day, from September 1 to Election Day. *Sources:* Raw data from Wisconsin Advertising Project and Wesleyan Media Project

So while television viewing in the middle of the day skews heavily Democratic, those viewers are far less likely to vote, which explains the dip in percentage of ads aired—for both Democratic and Republican candidates—during those hours.

The second lesson from Figure 5.4 concerns differences across parties. Republicans disproportionately advertise more during prime time and less during the early afternoon than Democrats. This also comports with the pattern of viewership we mentioned earlier. Daytime television viewers skew Democratic, so Democrats have more opportunities to reach voters over the course of the day, which is why their advertising is slightly more spread out. These differences are apparent in both the 2012 and 2014 data, but it is important to keep in mind that these disparities are not overly stark. Republicans and Democrats see their advertising rise and fall over the course of the day in roughly the same fashion. Targeting by time of the day is apparent in the data, but it is less frequent than one might think.

Finally, let's look at the differences across the sponsors of political ads in terms of targeting. Consider recent presidential elections. Barack Obama's campaigns have been widely touted as revolutionary in their targeting of television ads and other campaign messages. His data analytics team heavily leveraged information on voters to target ads in various ways. Even though Republicans were leaders in the use of microtargeting advertising in 2004, they have lagged behind Democrats in recent elections, a fact that is not lost on the party's operatives. The data confirm these differences.

Looking at the sponsors of ads for the 2012 presidential campaign that appeared on news shows (as shown in Figure 5.2, that was about 55 percent of all ads for that election), the types of sponsors and the percent of all their ads that aired during news shows break down as follows:

- Obama campaign (46 percent)
- Pro-Obama super PACs (47 percent)
- Republican National Committee (57 percent)
- Romney campaign (62 percent)
- Pro-Romney super PACs (64 percent)

These data suggest that the Obama campaign and its equally data-conscious super PACs were more sophisticated in their hunt for specific types of voters, seeking out voters on a diverse range of programs, while the Romney campaign and Republican super PACs concentrated their ads on local news, the default option.

There is a lot that the ad data reveal about targeting between 2000 and 2014. Some of the data clearly point to more-sophisticated ad targeting by candidates and other political ad sponsors. The ability to reach subconstituencies on programs with a particular viewer profile is an important tactic for campaigns. On the other hand, the prevalence of ads on news broadcasts—and the relative infrequency of ad imbalances on many genres of television programming—suggest that many ads on local broadcasts are not yet purchased in a finely targeted way.

CONCLUSION

Campaigns have many options for where to place their ads, from local broadcast television and local cable to national network and national cable. The purchase of airtime for political advertising is becoming a more targeted process, and local cable ad revenues are increasing, but local broadcast remains far and away the dominant venue through which campaigns advertise.

Buying airtime to target particular voters will only get more sophisticated in future elections. While media buyers may continue to play an important role, purchasing political advertising is likely to become more of an automatic process, in which campaigns set limits for how much they are willing to spend to reach particular demographic segments through a dashboard, and automated systems auction off airtime to the highest bidder—similar to the way online advertising is currently purchased, or the way one might purchase stocks in the financial markets. And with the advent of addressable satellite television, for example, targeting ads to specific households is not far off. (In fact, online advertising can already reach individual voters instead of individual households.) As technology continues to evolve, the options available to campaigns will expand dramatically. We discuss these developments more in the next chapter.

There is a point to be made here, though, about the next steps in ad targeting research. To date, only a handful of studies have examined whether the content of political messages varies across intended audiences, mostly by examining campaigns' direct-mail efforts,[29] though there has been work examining the strategic use of women's voices in advertising.[30] As ad targeting develops on television and as campaigns utilize these options with greater frequency, it will be important to track the varied messages sent to voters. Do ads targeted to male voters on golf shows emphasize different issues than ads targeted to women voters on reality shows?

The development of ads aimed not just at broad categories of voters but at very small, specific audiences depends on the ability of campaigns to produce content that varies in multiple ways. New and varied content is not hard to imagine, but campaigns still say that the bottleneck in more targeting is at the creative level. Producing twenty-five different ads aimed at twenty-five different types of voters is not a task that most campaigns are equipped to do at this point, so we may still be a few election cycles away from seeing this type of targeting in great frequency. Still, some movement in that direction has been visible. The Obama campaign in 2008, for instance, slightly altered numerous political ads that aired in different states to provide the primary or caucus information for that state. An ad about Barack Obama's foreign policy credentials that aired in Texas before the state's Democratic caucus, for instance, ended with information about when the polls were open and what number to call for more information. The identical ad aired prior to the North Carolina primary but ended with that state's election information and the URL for a state-specific Obama website. Some content can be tweaked easily and quickly, but campaigns are still learning how to do that in real time.

A final point on ad targeting speaks to the broader implications of a targeting strategy taken to its extreme. One potential benefit of advertising is that it remains—in a world where voter targeting is still limited—one way by which voters of all political stripes (Democrats and Republicans) and interests (voters and nonvoters) can hear from candidates on both sides of the aisle. When an ad is "broadcast" in that sense, it is perhaps "wasted" on certain voters who will never vote for that candidate or never vote at all, but the message is heard nonetheless and the electorate may be better informed as a result.[31]

In fact, if scholars like Markus Prior are right and the development of cable television and the proliferation of entertainment media have encouraged citizens to expose themselves only to those news programs with which they agree—or to stop following politics entirely—ads might be the only means left through which candidates talk broadly to a wide audience. Of course, ads will be less able to fill the gap in information availability if microtargeting efforts expand. Thus, political advertising may soon further reinforce differences between the parties and may contribute to polarization. It is important to remember, though: we have not yet reached that extreme.

DISCUSSION QUESTIONS

1. What are the advantages and disadvantages of placing ads on local broadcast television instead of local cable television? How do these change when the election is for president or governor, or for local office?

2. How might the correspondence of media market borders and congressional district lines influence the amount of campaign information that voters living in certain areas are exposed to? Are certain voters, in a sense, disadvantaged by living in a certain media market and not an adjacent one? How?

3. Targeting ads to specific television networks and programs allows campaigns to speak to just about any type of audience they want. If you were a campaign consultant, which groups of people would you want to send messages to? Just your supporters? Why or why not? What are the consequences of your choice for democracy?

4. Making decisions about which shows to air ads on requires a fair amount of work collecting information of viewer demographics. What are the advantages and disadvantages of simply airing most ads on news programs?

NOTES

1. Living in a county officially assigned to a media market by Nielsen does not mean that that everyone living in that county watches television stations based in that media market. Especially near the edge of media markets, viewers may get television signals—and cable feeds—from stations in multiple adjacent media markets.

2. "Local Television Market Universe Estimates," TVB Local Media Marketing Solutions, September 27, 2014, http://www.tvb.org/media/file/Nielsen_2014-2015 _DMA_Ranks.pdf.

3. Travis N. Ridout, "The Market Research, Testing and Targeting Behind American Political Advertising," in *Political Marketing in the United States,* eds. Jennifer Lees-Marshment, Brian Conley, and Kenneth Cosgrove (New York: Routledge, 2014), 220.

4. Elizabeth Wilner, "'On Points:' Local Cable Could Claim 25% of Political TV Ad Spending in 2014," *Cook Political Report,* October 29, 2013, http://cookpolitical .com/story/6381.

5. Ridout, "The Market Research, Testing and Targeting Behind American Political Advertising."

6. See, for example, the discussion of these data in Thomas B. Edsall, "Let the Nanotargeting Begin," *New York Times,* April 15, 2012, http://campaignstops .blogs.nytimes.com/2012/04/15/let-the-nanotargeting-begin/.

7. One answer with respect to sports programming is that the audience profile can vary across sports: viewers of auto racing are not typically viewers of golf or tennis. Still, on balance, Republicans watch more sports than Democrats.

8. Ridout, "The Market Research, Testing and Targeting Behind American Political Advertising."

9. Eitan Hersh, *Hacking the Electorate: How Campaigns Perceive Voters* (New York: Cambridge University Press, 2015).

10. The Cancel Bear, "Where Did the Primetime Broadcast TV Audience Go?," *Zap2it,* April 12, 2010, http://tvbythenumbers.zap2it.com/2010/04/12/where-did -the-primetime-broadcast-tv-audience-go/47976/.

11. The definition of *network* has changed over the years. Traditionally, this term referred to ABC, NBC, and CBS. Fox was added in the early 1990s, and the WB and UPN were added around 1999. The WB and UPN combined to form the CW in 2006. Telemundo and Univision, two Spanish-language networks, are also included currently.

12. Experian, *Cross-Device Video Analysis,* 2015 report, (based on Spring 2014 Simmons data), accessed June 17, 2015, http://www.experian.com/marketing -services/cross-device-video-analysis.html.

13. Markus Prior, *Post-Broadcast Democracy: How Media Choice Increases Inequality in Political Involvement and Polarizes Elections* (New York: Cambridge University Press, 2007).

14. Natalie Jomini Stroud, *Niche News: The Politics of News Choice* (New York: Oxford University Press, 2011).

15. The Cancel Bear, "Daily Television Viewing by Household 1952–2007," *Zap2it*, August 28, 2007, http://tvbythenumbers.zap2it.com/2007/08/28/daily -television-viewing-by-household-1952-2007/291/.

16. Pew Research Center, *In Changing News Landscape, Even Television Is Vulnerable*, September 27, 2012, http://www.people-press.org/2012/09/27/in -changing-news-landscape-even-television-is-vulnerable/.

17. Kenneth Olmstead, Mark Jurkowitz, Amy Mitchell, and Jodi Enda, "How Americans Get TV News at Home," Pew Research Center, October 11, 2013, http://www.journalism.org/2013/10/11/how-americans-get-tv-news-at-home/.

18. Wilner, "'On Points:' Local Cable Could Claim 25% of Political TV Ad Spending in 2014."

19. Bill Carter, "Republicans Like Golf, Democrats Prefer Cartoons, TV Research Suggests," *New York Times*, October 11, 2012, http://mediadecoder.blogs .nytimes.com/2012/10/11/republicans-like-golf-democrats-prefer-cartoons-tv -research-suggests/.

20. We hand-coded each unique program into these larger categories.

21. Travis Ridout, Michael Franz, Kenneth Goldstein, and Will Feltus, "Microtargeting Through Political Advertising," *Political Communication* 29, no. 1 (2012): 1–23.

22. Luke Rosiak, "In Pursuit of Coveted Independents, Campaign Ads Invade Local TV News," *Washington Times*, September 2, 2012, http://www .washingtontimes.com/news/2012/sep/2/in-pursuit-of-coveted-independents -campaign-ads-in.

23. Pew Research Center, *Americans Spending More Time Following the News*, September 12, 2010, Section 1, http://www.people-press.org/2010/09/12/section-1 -watching-reading-and-listening-to-the-news/. The survey reports the percentage of viewers who "regularly watch local television news."

24. Moreover, on average strong Democrats watch television at higher rates than Republicans. The gap in viewership between partisan groups is lowest during early evening, when local news shows are most prominent. As such, political ads on local news are one means by which Republican candidates can talk to more Republican television viewers. By implication, though, Democratic voters are still exposed to these messages, since they also watch the news in addition to watching throughout the day. Data on television viewership by time of day was provided by political consultant Will Feltus, who has analyzed polling data

through Scarborough Research. The underlying chart that demonstrates these trends is available on request from the authors.

25. The figure shows the number of ads aired on behalf of Democratic and Republican congressional candidates in 2014 (across ad sponsors) for dozens of program genres. These included a variety of sports programs, from horse racing to golf, variety shows, game shows, local news, sitcoms, mystery shows, and so on. The genres were ranked from low to high on the percentage of ads aired on behalf of Democrats.

26. Lydia Saad, "TV Is Americans' Main Source of News," *Gallup*, July 8, 2013, http://www.gallup.com/poll/163412/americans-main-source-news.aspx.

27. Data collected by Scarborough Research from February 2010 to March 2011.

28. Nielsen, *What a Difference the Day(Part) Makes*, April 2, 2013, http://www.nielsen.com/us/en/insights/news/2013/what-a-difference-the-day-part--makes.html.

29. D. Sunshine Hillygus and Todd G. Shields, *The Persuadable Voter: Wedge Issues in Presidential Campaigns* (Princeton, NJ: Princeton University Press, 2014).

30. Patricia Strach, Katherine Zuber, Erika Franklin Fowler, Travis N. Ridout, and Kathleen Searles, "In a Different Voice? Explaining the Use of Men and Women as Voice-Over Announcers in Political Advertising," *Political Communication* 32, no. 2 (2015): 183–205.

31. We use "heard" here to indicate exposure only. There is a debate in the field about whether political ads can persuade voters of the other party. Some of our work on this question suggests that ad effects are not confined to like-minded partisans and/or swing voters, but others suggest that political ads generally reinforce partisanship rather than soften it. Regardless of which is true, a precondition of persuasion is exposure, and the ability of partisans to see messages from the opposition is no small thing.

CHAPTER 6

The Internet, Social Media, and Advertising

On April 12, 2015, Hillary Clinton announced her presidential bid in a two-minute video uploaded to YouTube and posted on her website. The video featured upbeat music and a variety of different "everyday" Americans discussing their preparations for major life changes—moving, starting a business, going back to the workforce, having a baby, retiring, and so on. Clinton appeared roughly ninety seconds into the spot, saying, "I'm getting ready to do something, too. I'm running for president." On May 4, 2015, Carly Fiorina announced her own presidential campaign in another YouTube video. The first thing that Fiorina did after appearing on-screen was to turn off Hillary Clinton's announcement, which was playing on a television in the background.[1]

Several years ago, launching a presidential bid through a YouTube video was seen as innovative, but today, it is par for the course. Indeed, campaigns are increasingly using multiple online and social media tools to reach voters to boost the reach of their advertising. **Social media** refers to online platforms that allow individuals to create and share content as well as view and comment on other users' content, whether text, images or video. If the 2006 election was the "social media test run," 2008 cemented social media as "standard procedure for campaign websites."[2] In some cases, this social media outreach simply mirrors the messages featured in television advertising, but in others, the messages differ a bit from television because of differences in the audience for each platform and differences in the platforms themselves.

In this chapter, we will examine three major social media platforms—YouTube, Facebook, and Twitter—and how they have been utilized by campaigns. We also discuss the impact that online advertising has had on campaigns and ponder the impact that this growing form of advertising might have on future campaigns and elections. Before we delve into discussion of each social media tool, however, it is worth pausing to note that there are two distinct types of online and social media outreach: earned online media (sometimes referred to as *organic reach* or *user-generated content,* UGC) and paid online media. **Earned online media** refers to the dissemination of campaign messages through social media users who watch and share videos, images, or other messages, post and "like" them on Facebook, or retweet them on Twitter. **Paid online media**, by contrast, refers to campaign efforts to reach audiences by purchasing advertising on social media platforms. This could take the form of a **pre-roll ad** (an ad that appears before viewers watch an unrelated YouTube video or see content on a website), an ad on the side of a website, a sponsored box on Yahoo!, an ad in Facebook news feeds, or a promotional tweet or video in Twitter feeds.

PAID ONLINE MEDIA

There are many different types of online paid advertising, in part because citizens use multiple devices—personal computers, tablets, and mobile phones—to access the web. Google's Politics & Elections ad toolkit alludes to these three devices, in addition to traditional television, with its slogan, "Four screens to victory."[3] But it is even more complicated than that because there are multiple platforms on the web through which campaigns can purchase advertising. For example, Google sells advertising on Facebook as part of its own inventory, but campaigns can also purchase advertising directly through Facebook. In this section, we will discuss the different types of online advertising campaigns can purchase, beginning with those that have been around the longest.

The first type of online advertising was the **banner ad**, and it still exists today. It is a large advertisement that appears across a website (usually the top) and encourages viewers to click to see the advertised content. Banner ads fit under the broader category of **display advertising**, which is advertising that relies primarily on images, audio, and/or video to convey their messages. Display ads can appear as banners across a page or in smaller boxes throughout a website. Display advertising for campaigns can be tailored to appear on sites with related content (for example, on the side of political stories in an online newspaper), but they do not have to be targeted this way. Display advertising can also be purchased for **remarketing** purposes, where campaigns can advertise to individuals who have previously visited their website (or searched for their candidate) but have not yet taken a specific action (like donating money or signing up to receive e-mails).

Search advertising is a type of advertising purchased by campaigns that is tailored to your search behavior. When you type "Rand Paul"—or any other presidential candidate's name—into Google, for example, paid advertising links are likely to be among the first links to appear, directing you to "join the campaign" by signing up for an e-mail list or to "support the candidate" by donating money. These links are likely to appear early after a candidate announces but will vary depending upon the searcher's demographic profile and geographic location and candidate presets about the types of individuals to whom they would like to advertise. Campaigns use this type of advertising to pursue **online acquisition**, which is sometimes also called *direct response,* in an effort to capture personal contact information, including e-mail or mailing addresses, from individuals. Here the goal is to convert your search behavior into action—joining an e-mail list or donating money—so the campaign can keep track of you and provide you with additional information over the course of the campaign. Search advertising does not have to be in the form of textual links; display or pre-roll advertising can also be served to users based on their keyword search behavior, geographic location, and demographics.

Purchasing television ads is challenging given the growth of targeting on multiple channels, media markets, and time periods, but the unlimited possibilities of targeting on the web make the process of purchasing online ads even more difficult. The latest invention in online advertising is **programmatic advertising**, which is designed to make online targeting easier. Much as the stock market allows for automated transactions, programmatic advertising automates the process of selling ads by enabling real-time bidding from campaigns based on preset parameters. For example, the Hillary for America campaign could specify that it wants to bid on all opportunities to advertise to users who are thirty-five and under, live in Denver, Colorado, and search for "election" in their browser. The campaign can predetermine how much it is willing to pay for these opportunities based on the type of ad space available (for example, display or search), the prominence of the ad space, and whether or not a video can be skipped.[4] Although programmatic advertising is not entirely new, it is predicted to be a large growth market for advertising in 2016. In addition, companies that specialize in selling programmatic ads recognize that campaigns are accustomed to reserving inventory months in advance and thus are giving campaigns those same opportunities with programmatic ad space.[5]

Although we know that campaigns do a lot of paid online advertising, it is incredibly difficult to track—even for campaigns themselves. One reason for this is that although television advertising is highly regulated (both in terms of reporting requirements for expenditures and a mandate for a clear and legible disclaimer in the ad itself), online advertising activity is not. Campaigns must report expenditures for online ads only if the ad cost money to place. Banner ads, for example, must contain disclaimers, and the cost to place the ad is reported to the Federal Election Commission. But efforts to promote earned online media are unregulated, as are ads posted and displayed on one's website and videos available on a candidate's YouTube channel or Twitter feed. Moreover, outside groups can avoid all reporting requirements for their online efforts if they buy or freely promote the types of "issue advocacy" messages we discussed in Chapter 2. As such, dark money groups that can hide from the Federal Election Commission the identity of the donors who paid for their television ads can also hide the sponsorship of their online ads, and even the ad itself can go largely unnoticed by the FEC and the media if the sponsor can claim it is issue advocacy.

Another reason paid online advertising is challenging to track is that the detailed personal information about online users that search engine and social media companies collect allows them to sell very targeted advertising to campaigns. The upshot is that different users see different ads based on their demographic characteristics. Campaigns provide online and social media companies or third-party vendors for those companies with lists of people they want to target from their voter files. The companies attempt to match their user profiles to the list via e-mail addresses (for companies like Facebook that have that information) or browser cookies and IP addresses (for search engines like Google). To help protect privacy, however, there is always a wall between the advertiser (in this case, the campaign) and the companies selling the ads. The only information the campaigns get back from the companies is how good the "match rate" is between the list and the users of the platform. In other words, the campaigns never know who exactly from their list received their advertising. They simply receive information about the percentage of their list that matched along with some high-level demographic information—for example, that there is a 45 percent match rate, and 48 percent of that matched list is female. To verify that the advertising they purchase is being seen, campaigns frequently include a few of their own employees on the list, allowing them to monitor how the ads appear on their browsers. But the underlying point is that not even campaigns know exactly who from their desired list receives the advertising they purchase.

EARNED ONLINE MEDIA

Due to the difficulty of tracking paid online advertising, we will focus mostly on earned social media outreach and user-generated content (UGC), in particular on YouTube, Facebook, and Twitter. These are not the only platforms: Instagram, Snapchat, and Vine, among others, are growing and may represent new areas for campaign innovation. And in fact, the existence of multiple growth platforms further underscores the extent to which advertising in the modern campaign arena is becoming increasingly fragmented.

YouTube

YouTube is the most prominent video-sharing website in the world and is the home of the vast majority of online streaming videos.[6] Today, almost all US senators and members of the US House of Representatives have official YouTube channels on which they post videos,[7] but that was not always the case. YouTube was first used in election campaigns in 2006, but very few candidates that year had their own YouTube channels. Only 10 percent of Senate candidates had YouTube channels, and that percentage was even lower for House candidates.[8]

The use of YouTube in campaigns took off in 2008 as more campaigns began to create and post online video. Campaigns also expanded the ways in which they used video. Instead of creating videos that resembled ads seen on television—or just posting ads that also aired on television—campaigns tried different formats and used online video for a variety of purposes. Campaigns have taken advantage of the ability to post lengthier videos on YouTube to include entire speeches or rallies. Some campaigns have also created YouTube videos to better personalize their candidates.[9] Such videos focus on the character of the candidates—and getting to know the candidates as people—as opposed to the candidates' political experience or issue stances. One good example of this is a video posted by the Obama campaign in 2008 that featured Craig Robinson, Obama's brother-in-law, discussing Barack's style on the basketball court. This was interspersed with images of Obama shooting baskets. Campaigns hope that their online videos will go viral so that thousands, if not millions, see the ad. If this happens, it also may garner additional media attention.

Another development in 2008 was the increasing prominence of user-generated videos. Candidates and other political actors were not the only ones posting videos. Celebrities, comedians, and even everyday citizens created political videos, some of which went viral. The best example of this is the "Yes, We Can" video, which consisted of the words of an Obama speech set to music, shown against black-and-white images of the future president. The song was produced by will.i.am of the Black Eyed Peas and was viewed online over thirty million times.[10]

Given the many different sponsors of online campaign videos, and the many different formats they take on, it is fair to ask: What qualifies as an "ad" online? Does almost every video that mentions a candidate qualify? Or should we narrow it down to only those videos that closely resemble the political ads seen on television? There is no right answer to these questions, but one good guideline is that for an online video to count as a political ad, it must: (1) mention the name of a candidate, (2) be designed to persuade undecideds or mobilize supporters, and (3) be edited or scripted in some way. Thus, posting a twenty-three-minute-long speech given by a candidate would not qualify because it is not edited or scripted, and posting a news story about a campaign event would not qualify because it was not designed to persuade.

Why do candidates and other actors in campaigns use online video? One reason is that it is cheap. A campaign staffer with inexpensive video editing software and some technological savvy can produce and post an online ad, whereas developing a television ad usually takes the services of a media production company, not to mention the cost of purchasing airtime. Second, posting an ad online can be done quickly. If an important event happens or a candidate makes a gaffe, the campaign can post its response online within hours, whereas it would take days to do so with television advertising. The quickness of the response also means that campaigns have the ability to try to set the narrative for news reporters. For instance, right after 2012 vice presidential debate, the Republican National Committee put out a web video showing Democrat Joe Biden smiling and laughing while Paul Ryan talked about serious issues, including job growth and Iran. The message they were trying to convey to reporters and the public was that Biden was a bit daffy and frivolous—certainly not as serious as he should be when it comes to the big issues facing the country. Posting videos online also gives campaigns a better opportunity to speak to younger voters, who are much more likely to be online and using social media than older individuals. In January of 2014, 89 percent of those ages eighteen to twenty-nine reported using social media, compared to just 49 percent of those age sixty-five and older.[11] By contrast, older people are much more likely to be watching news programs on television—where many ads run—than younger people.

Let's take a deeper look at the way campaigns utilize YouTube and consider the ads posted there during the 2012 presidential race between Obama and Mitt Romney. We examined television ads aired by eight different sponsors and ads posted to the official YouTube channels of those same sponsors between September 1 and Election Day.[12] Those sponsors were the Obama and Romney campaigns, the Republican Party, the Democratic Party, Restore Our Future (a Romney-supporting super PAC), Priorities USA Action (an Obama-supporting super PAC), and American Crossroads and American Future Fund (two conservative groups). Table 6.1 shows the number of unique ads aired by each sponsor on television and the number of ads (as defined earlier) that each sponsor posted on YouTube. Many of the ads designed for television were also posted on YouTube, but we excluded those from the YouTube ad totals.

The table shows, first, that candidates sponsored the most television ads: eighty-four from Obama, sixty-seven from Romney. But Obama's campaign was far more active online, posting seventy-six videos to Romney's twenty-eight. The political parties, on the other hand, were much more active online than on television in the presidential race. In 2012, the parties focused their television advertising in down-ballot races, letting the presidential nominees raise their own money to pay for ads (or letting outside groups pay for them).[13] On the other end of the spectrum, the super PACs Priorities USA Action and Restore Our Future focused solely on television advertising and did not create any original online content.

If we look beyond the largest sponsors to all ad sponsors in the presidential race from September 1 to Election Day, we see that the television ads were more negative than the online ads (see Table 6.2):

Table 6.1: Biggest Ad Sponsors in the 2012 Presidential Race, September 1–Election Day

Sponsor	TV ads	YouTube only
Obama campaign	84	76
Romney campaign	67	28
Republican Party	13	24
American Crossroads	12	7
American Future Fund	11	2
Priorities USA Action	9	0
Restore Our Future	9	0
Democratic Party	2	39
Total	**207**	**176**

Source: Wesleyan Media Project

56 percent of television ads were negative compared to 43 percent of online ads. On television, only 15 percent of ads were positive, compared to 38 percent online. The greater positivity in online advertising may be due to the multiple goals of its sponsors. Encouraging existing supporters to get to the polls or to donate money is often done with positive advertising, whereas negative appeals are more useful for persuasion, which is the central goal of television advertising. Still, there is substantial negativity online. Campaigns often try to create a negative image of their opponents through online advertising, and they hope that the news media will repeat these narratives in their coverage.

There are also differences between television ads and online ads with regards to their focus on policy (see Table 6.3). Three out of four television ads focus on policy, whereas only half of online ads have a policy focus. Interestingly, regardless of whether an ad is on television or online, there is little focus on the candidates' personality or personal characteristics. Fewer than 10 percent of ads, regardless of medium, focus primarily on the personal characteristics of candidates.

The interesting thing about online ads is that many of them (39.8 percent of the 190 ads we collected from the 2012 presidential race) addressed neither policy nor the characteristics of the candidates. Some

Table 6.2: Tone of 2012 Presidential Ads by Medium

	TV ads	Online-only ads
Positive	14.9%	38.4%
Contrast	29.0%	18.9%
Negative	56.1%	42.6%
Number of ads	262	190

Source: Wesleyan Media Project

Table 6.3: Policy Focus of 2012 Presidential Ads by Medium

	TV ads	Online-only ads
Personal	7.6%	4.2%
Policy	75.3%	50.3%
Both	15.6%	5.8%
Neither	1.5%	39.8%
Number of ads	259	190

Source: Wesleyan Media Project

focused on personal stories about people other than the candidates, such as the ad that showed a struggling owner of a furniture business in North Carolina describing how her community had suffered under Obama's presidency or the ad featuring a family who was volunteering for Obama's campaign. Others encouraged people to get out and vote. One Romney ad featured Romney telling voters to vote "for love of country," while an Obama ad showed First Lady Michelle Obama asking New Hampshire residents to confirm the location of their polling place.[14]

Which types of ads posted on YouTube have the most impact? One way to assess this is to examine the number of views and shares of each type of advertisement (see Table 6.4). Negativity is more appealing, attracting more shares and hits than contrast and positive ads. Indeed, while negative ads account for only 43 percent of online ads (see Table 6.2), they account for 60 percent of the shares and 50 percent of the hits. Positive ads appear to be the least engaging, getting only about

Table 6.4: Number of Shares and Views by Tone

	Shares	Views
Negative	602 (60%)	142,350 (50%)
Contrast	254 (25%)	105,589 (37%)
Positive	141 (14%)	36,068 (13%)

Numbers in parentheses are percentages of the column total. *Source:* Wesleyan Media Project

Table 6.5: Number of Shares and Views by Policy Focus

	Shares	Views
Policy	476 (30%)	127,429 (30%)
Personal	475 (30%)	158,153 (37%)
Both	420 (26%)	84,197 (19%)
Neither	229 (14%)	60,324 (14%)

Numbers in parentheses are percentages of the column total. *Source:* Wesleyan Media Project

one-fourth the shares and hits of the average negative ad, even though they account for 38 percent of online ads.

People are also more attracted to online ads that focus on either policy or the candidates' personal characteristics (see Table 6.5). Ads touching on personal characteristics are the real winner here, accounting for 30 percent of the shares and 37 percent of the hits, even though such ads were only 4 percent of the total online ads (see Table 6.3). Those that are about neither—such as get-out-the-vote messages or ads that focus on people other than the candidates—are the least engaging, getting only about half the shares and hits (which amounts to 14 percent of the total across ad types).

Facebook and Developments in Online Video

No social media advertising discussion would be complete without considering Facebook, as 58 percent of the US adult population and 71 percent of adult Internet users are on Facebook.[15] Facebook has played a role in elections since at least 2006, when the company promoted a new "Election Pulse 2006" feature that allowed candidates to promote their profile pages.[16] Since then, the social media giant has transitioned to candidate pages, with news feeds that allows for additional points of contact between the candidate and users. In addition, recent developments in Facebook's video capabilities, including an automatic play feature, has made direct uploading of video to Facebook skyrocket, and Facebook's algorithms also privilege video updates over text or photo updates in users' news feeds.[17] In 2015, Facebook had four billion video streams per day, four times the number from the previous year.[18] For the first time, YouTube has a real rival in the video streaming market.

Thus, smart campaigns are likely to focus on posting video directly to Facebook in addition to cross-posting campaign videos on YouTube to gain more views. The Facebook app also intersects with campaigns' pursuit of advertising designed for mobile platforms. Indeed, Facebook's quarterly earnings report from March 2015 reveals that nearly three-quarters of its revenue came from mobile advertising.[19] Facebook is actively developing mobile advertising platforms that will enable users to open an ad in full screen and manipulate its content (for example, you might be able to move the ad around to view objects from all sides),[20] which could further encourage campaigns to build interactive mobile tools on Facebook.

However, recent changes to Facebook policies will make earned social media outreach harder for campaigns than it has been in the past. In 2012, the Obama campaign encouraged more than one million of its supporters to install the campaign's Facebook app, which gave users the option of sharing their friends list with the campaign.[21] Opting in allowed the campaign to compare the friends list with its voter files, letting it make suggestions to its Facebook supporters about the friends with whom they should share messages from the campaign. The Romney campaign used this type of tool late in the 2012 campaign, and both parties took advantage of it in 2014. However, Facebook implemented new rules in spring 2015 that limit how much information third-party applications can access, which will render this type of tactic impossible for future campaigns.[22] Because this avenue has been foreclosed, campaigns may resort to more paid advertising on Facebook in 2016.

Twitter

Of the big three social media platforms, Twitter is the newcomer to the political campaign toolkit—and to the social media scene in general. Fewer people use Twitter than Facebook or YouTube—19 percent of the US adult population and 23 percent of adult Internet users, according to statistics from 2014.[23] However, Twitter has enjoyed success among key audiences like journalists, celebrities, and technology elites, making it a key resource for campaigns to communicate breaking news and to try to control campaign narratives. Unlike other social media platforms whose use was pioneered by Democrats, Republicans were the first to use Twitter effectively, as part of their campaigns in 2010.[24] Since then, Twitter has become a mainstay of campaign toolkits for Democrats and Republicans alike, though younger and better-financed candidates, especially those running for the Senate, are more likely to tweet.[25]

Using interviews with 2012 Obama and Romney campaign staffers, scholar Daniel Kreiss argues that the presidential campaigns well understood the power of Twitter and planned their Twitter strategies and responses to possible narratives well in advance of known political events such as debates.[26] The Obama campaign, for instance, drafted hundreds of tweets to be disseminated by Obama's Twitter account depending on what Romney said during the debate.

How similar, then, is campaigns' use of Twitter to their use of political advertising? In order to answer this question, we examined both tweets and ads posted or aired after August from every US Senate candidate in the 2014 elections. First, Figure 6.1 reveals a positive, though not particularly strong, relationship between tweet and ad volume—such that more ads are correlated with higher volumes of tweets. The relationship between the two is stronger for Democrats than for Republicans, but there are multiple cases in both plots where there is high ad volume but relatively few tweets. For example, Democrat Mark Warner from Virginia aired over ten thousand ads between

September 1 and Election Day but tweeted only two hundred times. Similarly, Republican Mitch McConnell in Kentucky aired more than sixteen thousand ads but posted only about two hundred tweets. This stands in contrast to Iowa Democrat Bruce Braley, who posted over one thousand tweets and aired over nine thousand ads, and Republican incumbent Pat Roberts of Kansas, who aired five thousand ads and issued one thousand tweets. Still, the underlying fit of the plot suggests that both message streams are pursued aggressively and simultaneously. The competitiveness of the race seems to be the key factor here in explaining the volume of both types of messages sent to voters.

Our comparison of advertising and tweets also found that there is more substantive issue content in advertising, which should not be surprising given the difficulty of packing much information into 140 characters. Figure 6.2 plots the proportion of ads aired by candidates that mention policy issues against the proportion of tweets that do. (That number does not include tweets whose only mention of an issue was in a link.) The figure scales the size of each plotted point to reflect the number of ads aired. If advertising and tweets were equal in issue content, we should expect to see the dots lining up on the diagonal line. It is clear from the graph that ads are primarily issue-based, while tweets are not. In only one case does the issue coverage of tweets exceed that of the candidate's ads, and in every other case the imbalance is *heavily* weighted to more issue coverage in ads.

There is a common public refrain that political advertising is noxious to ideal political discourse, that it detracts from the proper functioning of a democratic system. And there is a sense among many that the Internet (or perhaps social media more specifically) can serve to level the playing field for underfunded candidates by providing a platform for political expression. Admittedly, this latter argument seems more of a straw man these days, given Americans' nearly twenty years of experience with some form of politics online. Indeed, Figure 6.2 reminds us that political ads—for all their pithiness and negativity—have important policy content that is lacking in tweets.

All told, Twitter's future as an important platform in political campaigns seems secure. One reason is its elite user base—politically

Figure 6.1: Number of Tweets by Senate Candidates, 2014

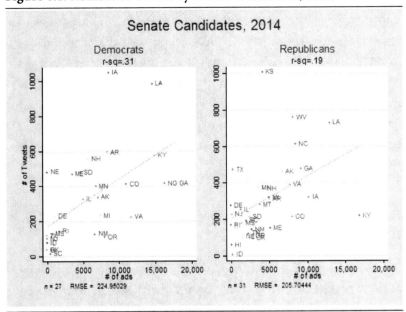

Plotted lines are the linear fits. *Sources:* Wesleyan Media Project and Twitter

Figure 6.2: Policy Content in Ads and Tweets by Senate Candidates, 2014

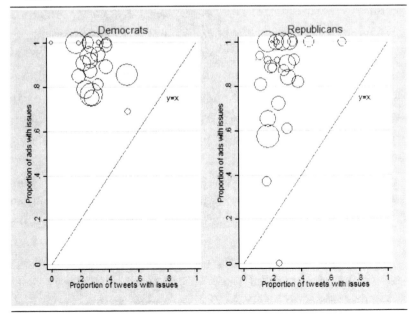

Entries are scaled by ad count across races. *Sources:* Data from Wesleyan Media Project and Twitter

knowledgeable and connected citizens whom campaigns want to reach. Another reason is that Twitter is changing to become more flexible. Much like Facebook, Twitter has recently invested in social video advertising and has recently made changes to allow real-time streaming and playback of video through an app called Periscope. Periscope's new mapping tool helps users find relevant geographical content and may make it much easier to use video with Twitter[27]—a development that campaigns are likely to embrace.

HOW ARE SOCIAL MEDIA PLATFORMS CHANGING CAMPAIGNS?

One great hope of the Internet and social media was that the advent of these new platforms would help candidates who were representing points of view not often heard in American politics and help break down the monopoly of the Democratic and Republican Parties. The idea is that a candidate with interesting ideas but without access to the resources provided by the political parties and their donor networks would be able to compete online, where Facebook pages, YouTube channels, and Twitter accounts are free. Certainly, one could name a few candidates in recent years whose support seemed to derive from online activities. Presidential candidate Ron Paul comes to mind. But most research on the topic finds that little has changed in the Internet era; traditional parties (and their candidates and supporters) still dominate campaign discussions.[28] Moreover, media coverage of online advertising overwhelmingly focuses on videos produced by traditional political actors.[29]

Another possibility is that the Internet, especially widespread video-streaming capabilities, has engendered creativity among ad producers, who are no longer limited to traditional advertising formats and thirty seconds of time. While one can point to examples of creative online videos that have gone viral, some scholars are dismissive of the idea that the Internet is a "game changer" when it comes to political advertising.[30] And so rather than a case of innovation, it may be more of a case of the same old campaigns (and same old power dynamics) moving to a new medium.

One result of the rise of the Internet is a possible bifurcation in the sources of campaign information for the young and the old, with younger people engaging in mobile social media and older people watching television. A potential concern resulting from this possible split is the lack of a shared campaign discourse. In other words, campaigns may be speaking to young people about one issue through online platforms while talking about different issues to older people through television advertising. If younger and older people are making their voting decisions based on different criteria, it could make it difficult for politicians to govern. On the other hand, the ability to speak in a different voice to different groups could be a positive if it allows campaigns to engage different groups of voters on the issues they care about the most.

CONCLUSION

This chapter has detailed the growth of advertising on the Internet and social media, examining the increasingly sophisticated ways in which campaigns use three of the most prominent social media platforms: Facebook, YouTube, and Twitter. Campaigns pay to get their messages out on each platform, but smart campaigns also use these platforms to earn free media as well, whether in the form of a share on YouTube, a retweet on Twitter, or a repost on Facebook. Campaigns hope these messages will disseminate not only to voters but also to reporters covering the campaign. Up to this point, though, the use of social media has complemented the use of television advertising rather than displacing it, and the types of candidates who do well in the Internet era seem not much different than those who did well in an earlier era.

Yet the use of the Internet and social media advertising continues to grow each year, which raises the question: can television advertising remain relevant? We think the answer is yes. For one, there are a lot of Americans—even young people—who still spend hours a day in front of their television screens, and thus television is still good for reaching a wide audience with a single message that a campaign wants to emphasize. If you want voters and the news media to be focused on one issue or theme, then television can be very effective. Second, most campaigns do not think of television and online advertising as mutually exclusive. Smart campaigns use both—sometimes to send complementary messages and sometimes to send different messages to different groups of people. Third, television advertising is adapting to the new environment. As the previous chapter discussed, campaigns are now better able to target television ads at specific sets of voters, making it much more attractive to advertisers.

At some level, the distinction between online advertising and television advertising may be narrowing. Many people are now watching programs disseminated by streaming video services, such as Hulu and Netflix, on Internet-enabled televisions. As more people cut the cord, this new way of reaching voters will surely become more prominent. We envision a future, then, in which campaigns advertise on broadcast television, cable television, streaming video, the Internet, Facebook, YouTube, Twitter, and the next new platform that has yet to be invented.

DISCUSSION QUESTIONS

1. In what ways have online advertising and social media changed political campaigns over the past decade, and in what ways are campaigns still the same? Would you say that campaigns are fundamentally different now or fundamentally the same? Why?

2. How is television advertising different from online advertising in terms of tone and content? Would you describe these differences as major? How might a heavy Internet user experience a campaign differently from a heavy television user?

3. Why do campaigns care so much about Twitter given that only a small percentage of Americans use the platform?

4. Compare the efficacy of television, Facebook, YouTube, and Twitter in reaching a large number of voters, in reaching politically sophisticated voters, and in reaching those who seldom vote.

NOTES

1. "Hillary Clinton Through the Years," TimesVideo, *New York Times,* April 12, 2015, http://www.nytimes.com/video/us/politics/100000003624500 /hillary-clintons-announcement-video.html; "Carly Fiorina Targets Hillary in Campaign Announcement Video," *Real Clear Politics,* May 4, 2015, http://www.realclearpolitics.com/video/2015/05/04/carly_fiorina_targets_hillary _in_campaign_announcement_video.html.

2. Stephanie Edgerly, Leticia Bode, Young Mie Kim, and Dhavan V. Shah, "Campaigns Go Social: Are Facebook, YouTube, and Twitter Changing Elections?," in *New Directions in Media and Politics,* ed. Travis N. Ridout (New York: Routledge, 2013), 88–99.

3. Google, *Politics & Elections Ads Toolkit,* accessed June 25, 2015, http://www .google.com/ads/elections/index.html.

4. Jeffrey F. Rayport, "Is Programmatic Advertising the Future of Marketing?," *Harvard Business Review,* June 22, 2015, https://hbr.org/2015/06/is-programmatic -advertising-the-future-of-marketing.

5. Kate Kaye, "Programmatic Buying Coming to the Political Arena in 2016: Broader Adoption Driving Interest Among Political and Advocacy Groups," *Advertising Age,* June 3, 2015, http://adage.com/article/digital/programmatic-buying -political-arena-2016/298810/.

6. Nielsen, *May 2012—Top U.S. Online Video Sites,* June 22, 2012, http://www .nielsen.com/us/en/insights/news/2012/may-2012-top-u-s-online-video-sites .html

7. L. D. Ricke, *The Impact of YouTube on US Politics* (Lanham, MD: Lexington Books, 2014).

8. Edgerly, Bode, Kim, and Shah, "Campaigns Go Social."

9. Scott H. Church, "YouTube Politics: YouChoose and Leadership Rhetoric During the 2008 Election," *Journal of Information Technology & Politics* 7 (2010): 124–142.

10. Edgerly, Bode, Kim, and Shah, "Campaigns Go Social."

11. Pew Research Center, *Social Media Use by Age Group Over Time,* http://www .pewinternet.org/data-trend/social-media/social-media-use-by-age-group/.

12. As mentioned earlier, to be considered an ad, an online video must mention a candidate, be designed to persuade undecideds or mobilize supporters, and be edited or scripted.

13. Recall from Chapter 3, however, that party advertising in Senate races (and to some extent also in House races) has been on the decline in the last fifteen years as outside groups continue to spend more in federal elections. We do not have comparable data on party-sponsored YouTube ads for House and Senate races.

14. Katrina Trinko, "Romney Ad: 'Vote for Love of Country,' Not 'Revenge,'" The Corner, *National Review,* November 3, 2012, http://www.nationalreview.com /corner/332401/romney-ad-vote-love-country-not-revenge-katrina-trinko; "First Lady Michelle Obama: Get Out the Vote New Hampshire and Confirm Your Polling Place," *Daily Motion,* July 7, 2015, http://www.dailymotion.com/video /x2x27e2.

15. Maeve Duggan, Nicole B. Ellison, Cliff Lampe, Amanda Lenhart, and Mary Madden, "Demographics of Key Social Networking Platforms," Pew Research Center, January 9, 2015, http://www.pewinternet.org/2015/01/09/demographics -of-key-social-networking-platforms-2/.

16. Edgerly, Bode, Kim, and Shah, "Campaigns Go Social.".

17. Erin Griffith, "How Facebook's Video-Traffic Explosion Is Shaking Up the Advertising World," *Fortune,* June 3, 2015, http://fortune.com/2015/06/03 /facebook-video-traffic/.

18. Ibid.

19. Kristine Lu, "Facebook's Deal with Publishers a Stark Reminder of Digital Ad Gulf," Pew Research Center, June 3, 2015, http://www.pewresearch.org/fact -tank/2015/06/03/facebooks-deal-with-publishers-a-stark-reminder-of-digital -ad-gulf/.

20. Martin Beck, "Facebook Unveils Vision for Immersive Mobile Ads," *Marketing Land,* June 24, 2015, http://marketingland.com/facebook-unveils-vision -for-immersive-mobile-ads-133335.

21. Jon Ward, "Facebook Shutting Down a Key Path Obama Used to Reach Voters," *Yahoo News,* November 17, 2014, https://www.yahoo.com/tech/s/facebook -slams-the-door-on-political-campaigns-212248365.html.

22. Colin Delany, "Facebook Kills a Grassroots Tool," *Campaigns and Elections,* July 30, 2014, http://www.campaignsandelections.com/magazine/1693 /facebook-kills-a-grassroots-tool.

23. Duggan et al., "Demographics of Key Social Networking Platforms."

24. Jeff Gulati and Christine B. Williams, "Communicating with Constituents in 140 Characters or Less: Twitter and the Diffusion of Technology Innovation in the United States Congress," *Social Science Research Network,* April 23, 2010, http://ssrn.com/abstract=1628247.

25. David S. Lassen and Adam R. Brown, "Twitter: The Electoral Connection?" *Social Science Computer Review* 29 (2010): 419–436.

26. Daniel Kreiss, "Seizing the Moment: The Presidential Campaigns' Use of Twitter During the 2012 Electoral Cycle," *New Media & Society,* December 5, 2014, 1–18.

27. Rose Pastore, "Twitter Just Made It Easier to Find Strangers' Videos on Periscope," *FastCompany,* June 4, 2015, http://www.fastcompany.com/3047066 /tech-forecast/twitter-just-made-it-easier-to-strangers-videos-on-periscope.

28. Eva Johanna Schweitzer, "Normalization 2.0: A Longitudinal Analysis of German Online Campaigns in the National Elections 2002–9," *European Journal of Communication* 26, no. 4 (2011): 310–327.

29. T. N. Ridout, E. F. Fowler, J. Branstetter, and P. Borah, "Politics as Usual? When and Why Traditional Actors Often Dominate YouTube Campaigning," *Journal of Information Technology & Politics* 3, no.2 (2015):237–251.

30. Ibid.

CHAPTER 7

Influence and Persuasion: Studying the Intended Effects of Advertising

It was 2008, and a Democratic presidential candidate had not won the state of Indiana in forty-four years—not since Lyndon Johnson's victory back in 1964. Four years earlier, in 2004, Republican George W. Bush carried 60 percent of Indiana's vote, compared to just 39 percent for Democrat John Kerry. And yet Barack Obama's campaign saw opportunity in the Hoosier State. They spent lavishly there, airing over eighteen thousand ads between September 1 and Election Day. The McCain campaign, by contrast, aired a little over one thousand spots in the state during the same time period, though that advertising was supplemented by advertising from the Republican Party. When all was said and done, Obama and his allies aired twice as many ads as McCain and his allies, and when the vote was announced on Election Day, Obama had won Indiana by the narrowest of margins. While Obama's huge advertising advantage was surely not the only factor contributing to his victory there, the unbalanced message flow—voters heard twice as many pro-Obama messages as pro-McCain messages—must have played some role.

We have spent a good deal of space in this book discussing how political ads are created, tested, purchased, and targeted, all with the fundamental goal of persuasion in mind. Given all of the attention campaigns pay to advertising, it seems reasonable to assume that it does indeed persuade and help candidates get elected. And yet early research had a difficult time uncovering any actual effect of advertising (or media propaganda more generally), and measuring the effects of advertising remains a complex and challenging process today. To understand better political advertising's influence, we begin by reviewing the history of persuasion studies and the major theories and challenges informing current research on media effects. Then we provide a broad discussion of the research methods and designs used to understand advertising's influence before turning to what we know today about how, when, and under what conditions advertising is likely to persuade.

THE HISTORY OF MEDIA INFLUENCE RESEARCH AND CURRENT CHALLENGES

Following the atrocities of World War II, there was great concern about the power of media influence and propaganda. Was it possible that Nazi propaganda had brainwashed German citizens? If so, the media were a very powerful force. In particular, there was apprehension based on the **hypodermic needle theory,** which was first posited in the 1930s and assumed that messages can be injected into the public in such a way that they will be automatically accepted and spread throughout society. In other words, the theory assumed audiences will passively accept the messages they receive.

The first studies of media influence in US elections in the 1940s, however, found nothing to support this theory. Using **panel data,** data collected by tracking individual voters' opinions over time, the researchers found remarkable stability in the opinions of voters and little evidence to suggest that campaign messaging changed minds.[1] This early work suggested that, far from being passive recipients of messages, audiences actively resist messages that are inconsistent with their **predispositions**—their preexisting opinions and political attachments—much more than previously thought. In addition, this work highlighted the notion of **selective exposure,** which is the idea that citizens actively seek out campaign information that confirms their predispositions and try to avoid messages that contradict them. This evidence, as well as the research done in the 1950s and 1960s, suggested that campaign messaging could have, at best, very minor influence on the public.[2] The idea that the effects campaigns have on voters are small has been called the **minimal effects model.**

The theory of minimal effects, however, did not stop campaign practitioners from continuing to produce messages to try to influence the public through media. In part because practitioners continued to use advertising—believing it to be effective—scholarly efforts to analyze the influence of political messaging rebounded in the late 1960s and 1970s.[3] One analysis of the 1972 election asserted that although political advertising changed the minds of only one to two in every one hundred voters, it was still better than the political coverage on national news broadcasts at providing information to those without a store of prior knowledge about the campaign.[4]

More recent work has made strides in both measurement and theory, in part because researchers acknowledge the inherent difficulties in detecting campaign effects and have worked hard to refine precisely where and under what circumstances we should expect to find them. More broadly, scholars now accept a theory of **conditional effects** (also known as *heterogeneous effects*), the notion that messages should not be expected to influence all citizens equally at all times and that their impact will vary depending on both the characteristics of the person who receives the message and the characteristics of the information environment.

One important reason that advertising effects are particularly challenging to uncover has to do with the pattern noted in Chapter 3: although the volume of advertising increases dramatically in competitive races, it tends to increase similarly on both sides as both campaigns compete to get their messages heard. In other words, the campaign message environment in competitive races tends to be characterized by **two-sided information flows:** both sides compete actively on air for citizen attention, attempting to equal or exceed each other's advertising volume.[5] When both sides are putting out the same number of messages, the influence of the competing messages is likely to cancel out. Therefore, to detect advertising influences, we need to look at situations in which one candidate has a considerable advertising advantage over his or her opponent, such as in Indiana in 2008.

Another challenge in assessing media influence has to do with the difficulties in measuring certain characteristics of audiences, specifically, their exposure to messages, their ability to understand messages (which affects the messages' reception), and their acceptance (or taking in) of messages. As we have already determined, individuals differ in their propensity to pay attention to ads, in their preexisting knowledge of politics, and in their political predispositions. All of these variables are challenging to measure, but perhaps none more so than **exposure**. Knowing what messages citizens are likely to have encountered is especially challenging in the real world because researchers frequently must rely on citizens' recollections of how much television they have consumed. Even if citizens accurately recall the number of hours of prime time programming they watched last week, researchers still have to approximate the number of ads to which they could have been exposed based on the average number of ads aired in the media market where they reside. This is a pretty rough estimate of an individual's exposure to advertising.

Further complicating these measurement issues is the fact that different people make different choices about which media to consume, which affects the content to which they are potentially exposed. Twentysomething Sarah, who gets most of her information from online sources, a mix of comedy news programs like *The Daily Show* and John Oliver's *Last Week Tonight,* and occasionally cable networks, is likely to see a different mix of advertising than forty-five-year-old Debbie, who watches daytime talk shows and local news.

Finally, even if Sarah and Debbie were exposed to the same advertising message, we cannot assume that they will have an equal reaction to the ad. **Political novices**, those who pay little attention to politics and do not seek out information about it, are much more prone to be influenced by advertising than **political sophisticates**, who spend a lot more time thinking about political information and have firmer preexisting attitudes as a result.[6] Evidence further suggests that other demographic characteristics—partisanship, race, gender, and class, for example—may also condition the influence that any particular message may have on political attitudes and opinions.[7]

WHAT WE KNOW ABOUT ADVERTISING'S ABILITY TO PERSUADE

The fact that the effects of ads are difficult for scholars to detect, for all the reasons discussed above, does not mean that ad effects do not exist, but we should not expect to find the large media effects that researchers in the 1930s hypothesized in the hypodermic needle model. Advertising mostly matters at the margin, but the margin is where most competitive races are won, which means that advertising effects—while not massive—can matter quite a bit. The trick to detecting ad effects is to look in the right place. In this section, we will look at the circumstances under which advertising can have a direct effect and be persuasive, focusing on differences in ad volume and content, and we will examine the influence ads can have indirectly through another source: the news media.

The Direct Influence of Political Advertising

As the Obama in Indiana example at the beginning of the chapter demonstrates, when a candidate has more ads on the air than his or her opponent, we tend to see increases in support for that advantaged candidate. For example, Figure 7.1 shows the number of ads aired in each House and Senate race between September 1 and Election Day, 2014, in each media market (each market is represented by a dot). Many of the dots are clustered around the 45-degree line, meaning that the number of pro-Democratic and pro-Republican ads is about equal in those markets. However, there were also many markets with imbalances of some significance.[8] Note, for example, that in almost every media market in House races, Democrats out-advertised Republicans. And yet Republicans won the national vote in these races (50.7 percent to 44.9 percent of all votes cast), and they picked up twelve additional seats, expanding their majority to 247 seats. Clearly, airing more ads than your opponent does not automatically mean you will win the race, but in a political environment like the 2014 election, in which Democrats faced headwinds, Democratic candidates' airing more ads than their Republican opponents may have mitigated their losses.

Campaigns spend a fair amount of time and effort on deciding the content and tone of their advertising. Do they have an impact on the persuasiveness of an ad? Quite a bit of research suggests that they do. Let's consider first the research around ad tone: are negative ads more influential than positive ads? Research suggests that negativity is more *memorable*,[9] but the evidence is less conclusive about whether negativity is more *persuasive* than positivity.[10] As we discussed in Chapter 3, negative ads can cause voter backlash against the sponsor, especially if the sponsor is the candidate. A negative ad may decrease people's evaluations of the opponent, but because citizens do not like negativity, their opinion of the favored candidate decreases as well. Therefore, the net persuasive effect of a negative spot—that is, the difference between the reduction in the candidate's favorability (due to a backlash) and the reduction in the opponent's favorability (due to the ad's attacks)—may not be that significant. For positive ads, since there is no backlash, the increase that the candidate gets may not need to be as large to equal the effect of a negative spot.

Content matters, too. As we noted in Chapter 3, campaigns tailor their messages to the themes or problems that are salient in a given year. For example, following the 2008 recession, ads for the 2010 midterm elections were predominantly about the economy. At a time when individuals and businesses were still struggling, messages about other issues may not have resonated with voters. The rise of microtargeting strategies suggests that campaigns are seeking ever-more-tailored methods of reaching voters. Evidence suggests that targeting can be an effective strategy for persuasion, as long as citizens don't know they are being targeted specifically, as voters say they dislike the idea of receiving tailored messages.[11] There are a number of studies on the content that different demographic groups prefer in political advertising— valuable information for campaigns to have. For example, some have found that advertising featuring ordinary Americans receives higher

Figure 7.1: Balance of Pro-Democratic and Pro-Republican Ads, September 1–Election Day, 2014

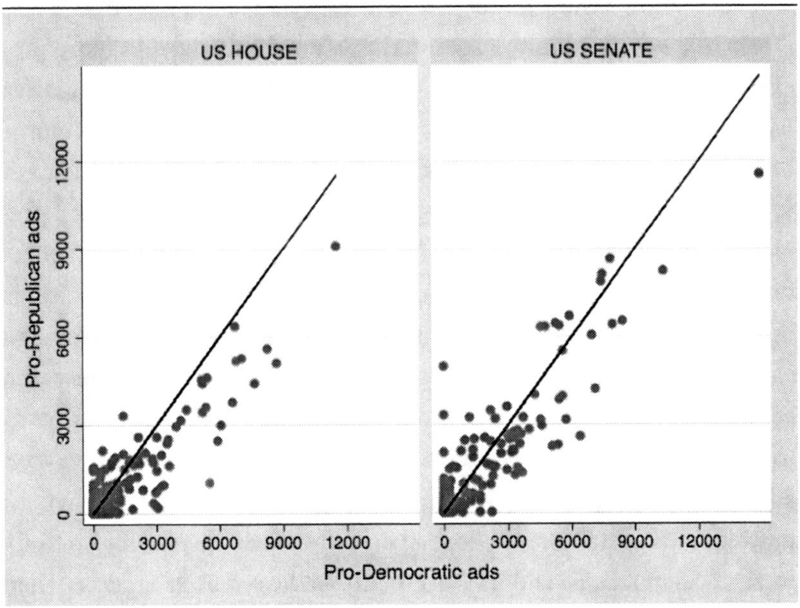

Each dot is a media market. *Source:* Wesleyan Media Project

ratings, especially among independent voters.[12] Another study discovered that partisans prefer to hear ads from their preferred candidates, whereas independent voters prefer to hear from independent groups.[13] And women find ads featuring women's voices to be more credible than men do.[14] We do not yet know the extent to which campaigns are tailoring the content of targeted messages—it is surely happening online, but it is likely less frequent on television. Still, one study found that ads featuring female voiceover announcers are more likely to air during programs with a larger female audience.[15]

Microtargeting does not come without risks, however, especially if citizens find out that two different messages are being sent to two different audiences. As noted above, the public dislikes the idea of tailored messaging, which can stir concerns of manipulation. Further, one study found that individuals who saw messages appealing to a group to which they did not belong were more likely to penalize the candidate for the "mistargeting."[16] Although the study examined visual cues online and not advertising in particular, it seems reasonable to suspect that the results might translate, especially if they are overt cues.

While advances in microtargeting allow campaigns to more precisely reach a target population, potentially increasing the persuasive influence of ads shown to that population, the growth in sheer volume of advertising may weaken the effectiveness of any individual ad or advertising advantage. Essentially, the first ten ads you view about a previously unknown candidate are likely to have much more of an effect on your opinion than the ten ads you see after you have already seen a hundred. This idea also suggests that earlier advertising in a campaign can be more powerful than later advertising; however, little research actually confirms this. In addition, advertising's persuasiveness tends to be short-lived.[17] In particular, research estimates that for most races, advertising effects decay quickly, lasting no more than five days. In presidential races, however, advertising effects may persist for up to six weeks.[18] So, if ad effects decay as quickly as the research suggests, then both early and late advertising are important and necessary.

Our own studies of ads and persuasion have led us to one important conclusion: lots of factors—perhaps too many to count—may condition advertising effects. Dozens of features of the ad content and the campaign environment are worth additional investigation, but we want to highlight one in particular: the type of race, which influences how well-known the candidates are. Studies have found that advertising advantages are especially beneficial in down-ballot races, where voters often know little about the candidates, and for challengers who often lack the same amount of name recognition as incumbents.[19] Thus, for presidential races, where voters are very familiar with the major-party nominees, given the nearly two years of primary campaigning preceding the general election, ads matter less in determining people's ballot-box choice. For US Senate races, where candidates are generally less known, ads have more of an impact, providing critical information to voters as they evaluate candidates.

We illustrate this in Figure 7.2, which shows how much the Democratic candidate's percentage of the vote increases when we (hypothetically) increase the ad advantage that the Democrat has over the Republican candidate by one standard deviation (a modest increase) in both presidential and Senate elections. The figure points to important differences between the two types of elections; the most apparent is the size of the effect. In presidential elections, the effect from a modest increase in ads is quite small, never reaching one percentage point, and the effect was even smaller in 2012. In Senate races, however, the effects are always larger, often exceeding three percentage points. But these effects can still vary quite considerably: in 2006 the effect exceeded four percentage points, whereas in 2014, the effect was only one and a half points. All told, even in Senate elections, the increase in votes due to an increase in ads is modest. The effect would likely be much larger, however, if one replicated this type of analysis in House races or lower-ballot races, where candidates are even less known than in Senate races.

Indirect Influence: Ad Amplification by the News Media

In the 2014 midterm elections, perhaps no ad was talked about more than Republican US Senate candidate Joni Ernst's "Squeal" spot. The ad featured Ernst walking through a barn, speaking directly into the camera. The signature line—"I grew up castrating hogs on an Iowa farm, so when I get to Washington, I'll know how to cut pork"—gained national attention due to its clever conjunction of Iowa farm values and eliminating government waste. The ad, which cost only nine thousand dollars to air but garnered extensive media attention and four hundred thousand views on YouTube the first three days after its airing,[20] helped Ernst to become well-known on the national political scene.

This ad is an excellent example of a phenomenon called **ad amplification**, also known as *free advertising* or *earned media*. This is a type of indirect influence that occurs when news media choose to cover a campaign ad, sometimes extensively, providing additional opportunities for citizens to take in the message of the ad. Earned media coverage of advertising is a common occurrence for three major reasons: (1) it is easy and inexpensive for journalists to cover since the ads in question provide plenty of material without the need to solicit

Figure 7.2: Increase in Votes Due to Increase in Ad Volume for the Democratic Candidate in a Presidential Race and a Senate Race

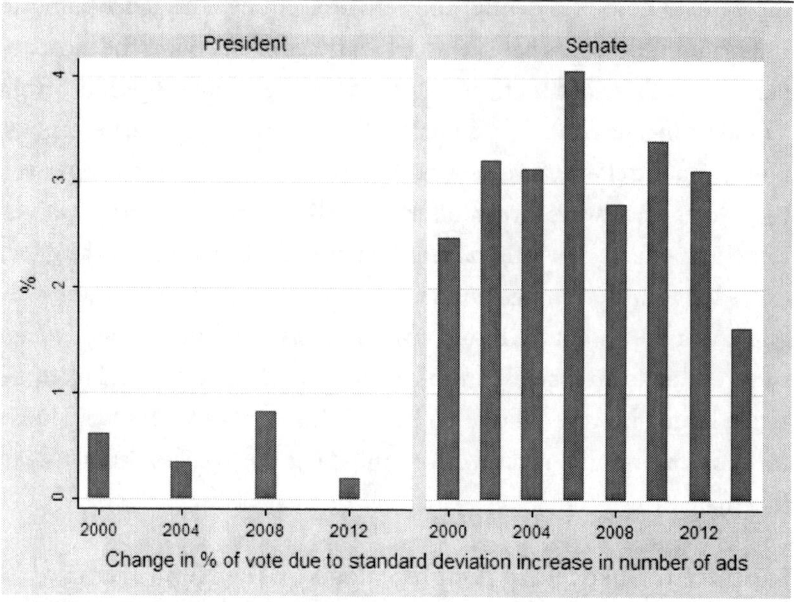

Estimates are from models of county vote as function of ads in October. Models control for demographic and political factors.

additional information or quotations from sources; (2) it fits with the journalistic norms of highlighting conflict and exposing inaccuracies; and (3) viewers like reading and watching **horserace coverage**, which can be easily tied to advertising and strategic tactics.[21] Horserace coverage is a type of news reporting that is focused on who is winning and losing a race—and whether a candidate is exceeding or failing to live up to expectations.

Research suggests that not only is ad amplification prominent during election season, it is also not a perfect reflection of the types of advertising on air at any given time. In particular, advertising that is negative in tone or particularly innovative is much more likely to get rebroadcast on television newscasts and to receive coverage in newspapers, and as a result, earned media coverage of advertising is more prevalent in competitive races.[22] As a consequence of the news coverage, citizens are even more likely to encounter negative advertising than they are other types of ads. This could amplify the benefits candidates get from negative advertising, though it could also mean that they receive greater backlash.

Media cover advertising for all kinds of reasons: to highlight the tone of the race, to discuss candidates' strategy and tactics, to evaluate an ad's factual claims, to highlight a policy issue or a character trait of a candidate, or to discuss how "successful" an ad has been. But research has shown that the majority of advertising coverage focuses on three of these: the ad's tone, the tactics and strategy behind its use, and whether its use was successful. Little coverage focuses on how accurate the advertising is (known as **adwatch coverage**) or on the policy or substantive issues mentioned in the ads.[23] Further evidence suggests that strategic coverage of advertising (encompassing tone, strategy, and character coverage) may drive up perceptions of campaign negativity, a topic to which we'll return in the next chapter.[24] Adwatch coverage is designed to correct misinformation, but most studies on the influence of adwatch coverage tend to find that it reinforces the memory of the ad's message rather than the reporter's evaluation of its accuracy.[25] A recent experiment, however, does show that politicians are less likely to make questionable statements if they know they are being monitored by the news media.[26] We will discuss adwatch coverage in greater depth in Chapter 8.

HOW DO WE KNOW WHAT WE KNOW? THE IMPORTANCE OF RESEARCH DESIGN

So far, we have simply summarized the research in political science on advertising persuasion without regard for the type of evidence used to corroborate the findings. But how exactly do we know that one ad is more effective than another or that individuals have been persuaded by advertising advantages? Scholars of political advertising use a variety of strategies to assess the influence of ads, and in this section we will outline three of them—the observational approach, experiments, and field experiments—along with examples of each type.

The Observational Approach

The first, and perhaps most straightforward, research design relies on what scholars call an **observational approach** to data; that is, researchers try to observe and measure real-world factors and then statistically control for elements they believe to be related to the outcome of interest—in the case of political advertising, vote choice or election outcomes. There are two basic types of observational designs, which vary in their **level of analysis**; that is, whether we observe and collected data on individuals or groups of individuals. The first is **aggregate-level analysis**, which examines groups of individuals. This might involve looking at state- or county-level vote returns to model the outcome of the election as a function of state or county demographics and the campaign activities (the number of ads purchased, for example) at that level.

We demonstrated the benefits of this approach in Figure 7.2, which examines the relationship between ad advantages and vote percentages for presidential and Senate races between 2000 and 2014. The advantage of estimating ad effects in this way is that it allows the use of real-world data for both the independent variable (ads aired) and the dependent variable (counted ballots), but there are also problems with this approach. For one, ad buys are not assigned randomly in the real world. In fact, the opposite is true: ads are bought strategically to reach swing counties in close races (or, in some cases, to shore up base counties with mobilization efforts). It is very hard to know if increased advertising makes a race more competitive, as Democratic appeals counter Republican appeals, or if a competitive race draws in more advertising. What we have demonstrated in the figure is clear correlation, but not obvious causation.

We tried to mitigate this **endogeneity**—a statistical problem that occurs when one variable is determined by another variable; because the variables likely affect each other, this makes it difficult to confirm causation—in our analysis in two ways. For Senate races, we controlled for a range of factors, including the presidential vote in the county (to take into account the county's ideological profile) and Senate-candidate spending in the state (to take into account competitiveness). Including these controls allows us to be more confident that the effects uncovered are due to advertising, not some other related factor. For the presidential effects analysis, we exploited the fact that media markets sometimes cross state lines, which allowed us to examine only counties in non-battleground states. Because media markets do not fit neatly inside of state lines, there are many counties in non-battleground states that border competitive states and thus receive "accidental" barrages of presidential ads. By only examining non-battleground counties that border battleground states, we are able to estimate the effects of advertising in states where the campaigns were not actively competing for Electoral College votes, and so we can be even more confident in the causal effects of the ads themselves in the presidential races. The estimated effect of ads on votes in these counties, then, amounts to a natural experiment of sorts, which gives us more confidence that we are uncovering the effects of advertising.

The second observational approach is called **individual-level analysis**. With this approach, researchers collect information on specific individuals' attitudes and opinions about advertising and/or the candidates in a particular race, along with other important variables such as how much media they consume, the content of the ads they are exposed to, and demographic characteristics, like race, sex, class, partisanship, and ideology. For example, several studies attempt to match individual citizens to the advertising that has aired in the media market in which they reside during the programs or the hours they report watching. So if an individual reports watching *Jeopardy!* every day but never reports watching local news, that person would be matched to all of the advertising aired on *Jeopardy!* in his or her media market but none of the ads aired on local television news. From that information, we have a fairly good sense of the balance of advertising to which a citizen may have been exposed and can look at whether advertising advantages correlate with his or her candidate preferences, controlling for the other factors known to influence persuasion.

The strength of these observational approaches is that they take advantage of the information we have in the real world, not data generated in a laboratory, and therefore they can be expected to generalize to other, similar conditions in the real world. Of course, one of the biggest weaknesses of observational methods is that they force us to rely on less-than-perfect—usually self-reported—measures of exposure to advertising, and studies have shown that citizens vary in their ability to accurately recall what television programs or advertising they have watched.[27] In the case of aggregate-level observational research, researchers have a hard time teasing out cause and effect, given the very strategic targeting of ads to places where the campaigns perceive the greatest need.[28]

Experiments

In contrast to observational research, **experiments** allow the researcher to control who receives the treatment (in this case, sees an advertisement) and who does not. Experiments were once conducted primarily in a research laboratory, which were often set up to mimic a living room, with some distractions available to the participant, like food or magazines, in addition to a television set. Today, however, many experiments are conducted via online surveys, in which survey participants are exposed to advertising on computers or electronic devices in their own homes.

The key to experimental design is **randomization:** individuals are randomly chosen to belong to the control group or treatment group. In other words, each participant in the survey has the same chance of being assigned to watch an advertisement or not to watch an advertisement. This helps to ensure that the individuals who see the ad are no different, as a group, than the individuals who do not see the ad. This way, an experiment overcomes the problem of selective exposure and other individual-level factors affecting persuasion and allows us to more definitively say that the difference we see in the two groups *after* exposure to the treatment is due to the treatment itself—seeing the ad—and not something else. Experiments also overcome the problem of self-reported media use because the researcher knows who has seen the ad and who hasn't. The weakness of experimental methods is that experiments can be somewhat artificial and may frequently overemphasize the real-world effects of ads, given that they are often tested in isolation without most of the real-world distractions that exist when a person encounters advertising.

One big advantage of experiments is that they allow researchers to directly compare the effects of individual components of advertising. For example, thanks to a series of experiments, we know that ads sponsored by unknown interest groups are more effective than ads from candidates.[29] In our own version of this type of experiment, we created two versions of the same ad—one said the ad was sponsored by one of the candidates and the other said the ad was sponsored by an interest group. Respondents were invited to participate in an online survey and then were randomly assigned to different treatment conditions. All participants read a description of a fictitious race in which two candidates were running. Basic information about the candidates was provided, and then depending upon their random assignments, some respondents saw the candidate ad, and some respondents saw the interest-group ad. Then all were asked a series of questions intended to assess how favorably the respondents viewed each of the candidates and for whom they would vote.

By comparing the responses of those who saw no ad to those who saw an ad, we could easily see that the ad itself was effective in lowering favorability of the candidate's opponent. By comparing the group who saw the candidate ad to the group who saw the interest-group ad, we could tell that the ad was more effective in moving opinions in favor of the candidate when it was sponsored by an interest group than when the candidate himself was seen sponsoring the ad. This sort of test would be impossible in the real world because candidates and interest groups run different advertisements—the experiment allows us to extricate the effect of the ad's sponsorship from the effect of the ad's content.

Field Experiments

Recently, scholars have started collaborating with campaign practitioners in running **field experiments**, which combine some of the benefits of an experiment—specifically, randomization—with observational tracking in the real-world ("the field"). Typically, campaigns allow the researchers to randomly assign one or more of the following: which media markets (and therefore which citizens) receive the advertising, when ads will appear, and how many of them there will be. In the first large-scale field experiment on persuasion, conducted in Texas during the 2006 gubernatorial election, Governor Rick Perry gave political scientists control of a two-million-dollar television and radio ad budget, which was used to air a positive radio and television spot in media markets in Texas. The researchers varied the ad's launch date and the number of airings in each market, which allowed them to compare effects across markets at the same time and within markets over time. They tracked citizen responses through a phone survey with one thousand registered voters every evening. Because of this research, we now know more definitively how advertising (or at least this specific positive ad) influenced voters. In this case, researchers discovered that the ad had a large but short-lived effect.

The biggest advantage of a field experiment is that it capitalizes on the strength of the experiment—the way randomization allows it to speak to causal influence—and examines effects in the real world, where we do not have to worry about the artificial nature of the laboratory or if the results will translate beyond the lab. Although field experiments represent perhaps the gold standard for research in the political campaign world, they are not without downsides. The first is cost. Field experiments are even more costly and time-intensive to plan than observational or experimental research, and as a result are often outside of the realm of possibility for many scholars unless they can find a campaign willing to forfeit control of advertising assignment for the sake of research. That prospect is challenging because campaigns are looking to win *this* cycle, not learn lessons for future ones. Further, although field experiments do improve upon experiments in laboratories, there are still, by necessity, simplifications. For all of the effort that went into the Texas field experiment, researchers still were only able to test the influence of a single ad. What if the ad had been a negative or contrast one? Would the effect have been different?

Finally, there are ethical considerations that come with conducting field experiments. Most previous field experiments in elections have not coordinated with a campaign but focused on turnout.[30] Trying to enhance turnout (and uncover which messages do so and to what extent) is seen as a public good. If the focus is election outcomes and shifts in votes towards one candidate, the treatment has most often focused on nonpartisan messages, such as encouragements to vote.[31] Field experiments like the one in the Texas—where the randomized treatment is a partisan message clearly meant to promote a candidate—are not common, and some, if done without the cooperation of a campaign, may be considered unethical. How much can researchers attempt to influence an election in the name of furthering academic knowledge?

In the fall of 2014, three political scientists launched a field experiment in a Montana race for the state supreme court.[32] The goal of the experiment was to see if providing information on the ideology of the candidates—whether they were liberal or conservative—via a mailer to a random sample of Montana households would affect voter turnout rates. But although the focus of the research was voter turnout, the message itself was considered by many to be too political—for example, the mailing revealed one candidate to be more liberal than Barack Obama. In addition, the mailing used an unauthorized copy of the Montana state seal, suggesting it was an official communication from the state. State officials objected to the use of the seal, and others argued that the underlying goal of the research was to influence the outcome of the election. Defenders of the experiment argued that the ideological information, which was calculated based on who donated to each candidate, was aimed at shedding light on how to improve democratic participation and engagement.[33] They also pointed out that practitioners conduct these sorts of experiments all the time.

The controversy makes clear that field experiments can be fraught with complications and challenges. Researchers would like to use this methodological approach to uncover the effects of negative ads, for example, but there is only so much that one can randomize in the real world of elections without possibly running afoul of election laws, critics who doubt one's intentions, or claims of improper influence.

CONCLUSION

Ideas about how influential political ads are have changed over time. At one point, scholars believed that political ads were a dangerous form of propaganda that could easily influence the masses. At another point, scholars believed that their effects were minimal given voters' defenses against them, such as selective exposure. Today, we tend to think that ads can have an influence—but only under the right circumstances and with the right individuals. Advertising influence is contextual; ads have more of an influence, for instance, when one side dominates or when voters know little about a candidate. With that in mind, campaigns will continue to seek out targeted opportunities to shape opinions and move voters. This may include a mix of massive television buys that saturate a market, along with microtargeting segments of the voting population and even specific individuals.

Today we are also more attuned to the indirect ways by which advertising can influence people, especially through amplification by the news media, which often cover and repeat the messages being sent by candidates and other ad sponsors. Often, however, the news media disproportionately cover negative advertising, giving audiences a false impression of how negative a campaign is.

Understanding advertising's influence requires employing multiple, creative research designs. Each approach, whether observational research at the individual or aggregate level, a lab experiment, or a field experiment, has advantages and disadvantages. Thus, the most thorough understanding of the effects of advertising is obtained by consulting multiple studies that use multiple approaches. Indeed, good science, and good political science, comes from the accumulation of insights gained through multiple studies, and we can be more confident in our scientific conclusions if multiple studies, with different ways of approaching the same question, find the same result.

Why should we care about understanding how much advertising influences people's votes? Certainly, there would be reason for concern if it were the case that political advertising could brainwash the public at large. Yet that's not the case. Advertising matters at the margin, generally moving support for federal candidates by fewer than four percentage points. Indeed, we have presented evidence suggesting that the persuasive influence of advertising may be declining over time, due to either oversaturation or changes in targeting, which means that fewer people "accidentally" see the advertising campaign designed to be shown only to the most persuadable targets.

At the same time, it is also true that some voters, some of the time, are influenced by political ads. If this influence occurs because voters are learning (accurate) information that they did not previously know—more on this in the next chapter—then advertising can actually be beneficial to voters. But if the influence is occurring because voters have only heard from one candidate because the other candidate cannot afford to purchase heavy volumes of advertising, or because a millionaire, corporation, or union funnels money to a super PAC for ads supporting that candidate, then there is more cause for concern.

DISCUSSION QUESTIONS

1. How has the history of studies of persuasion evolved, and why did scholars have so much trouble determining whether advertising was persuasive?

2. The news media frequently cover political advertising. Overall, is this a good thing in that it helps to keep candidates honest, or is it a bad thing in that it tends to emphasize the attacks contained in advertising? Can you think of other pros and cons of the news media's coverage of advertising?

3. What are some of the ethical issues surrounding the use of field experiments to study ad persuasion? Can these concerns be overcome? How?

4. How can observational research, experimental research, and field research complement each other in aiding our understanding of the persuasive influence of political advertising?

5. Are advertising's effects, as we uncovered them in Figure 7.2, too large, too small, or just about right? Why?

NOTES

1. Paul F. Lazarsfeld, Bernard Berelson, and Hazel Gaudet, *The People's Choice: How the Voter Makes Up His Mind in a Presidential Campaign* (New York: Columbia University Press, 1944); Bernard R. Berelson, Paul F. Lazarsfeld, and William N. McPhee, *Voting: A Study of Opinion Formation in a Presidential Campaign* (Chicago: University of Chicago Press, 1954); Angus Campbell, Philip E. Converse, Warren E. Miller, and Donald E. Stokes, *The American Voter* (Chicago: University of Chicago Press, 1960).

2. Doris A. Graber, "Political Communication: Scope, Progress, Promise," in *Political Science: The State of the Discipline II*, ed. Ada Finifter (Washington, DC: American Political Science Association, 1993).

3. Sidney Verba Nie and John R. Petrocik, *The Changing American Voter* (Cambridge, MA: Harvard University Press, 1976); Thomas Patterson and Robert McClure, *The Unseeing Eye: The Myth of Television Power in National Politics* (New York: Putnam, 1976).

4. Patterson and McClure, *The Unseeing Eye.*

5. John Zaller, "The Myth of Massive Media Impact Revisited," in *Political Persuasion and Attitude Change,* eds. Diana C. Mutz, Richard A. Brody, and Paul M. Sniderman (Ann Arbor, MI: University of Michigan Press, 1996), 17–78.

6. William J. McGuire, "Attitudes and Attitude Change," in *The Handbook of Social Psychology*, ed. G. Lindzey and E. Aronson, 3rd ed., vol. 2 (New York: Random House, 1985), 233–346; John Zaller, *The Nature and Origins of Mass Opinion,* Cambridge Studies in Public Opinion and Political Psychology (Cambridge, UK: Cambridge University Press, 1992).

7. Wendy Rahn, "The Role of Partisan Stereotypes in Information Processing about Political Candidates," *American Journal of Political Science* 37, no. 2 (1993); Nicholas A. Valentino, Michael W. Traugott, and Vincent L. Hutchings, "Group Cues and Ideological Constraint: A Replication of Political Advertising Effects Studies in the Lab and in the Field," *Political Communication* 19, no. 1 (2002): 29–48, doi:10.1080/105846002317246470; Patricia Strach, Katherine Zuber, Erika Franklin Fowler, Travis N. Ridout, and Kathleen Searles, "In a Different Voice? Explaining the Use of Men and Women as Voiceover Announcers in Political Advertising," *Political Communication* 32, no. 2 (2015): 183–205.

8. The totals in this graph collapse across sponsors on each axis. So all ads aired on behalf of the candidates, including from party committees and supportive outside groups, are included.

9. Ted Brader, *Campaigning for Hearts and Minds: How Emotional Appeals in Political Ads Work* (Chicago: University of Chicago Press, 2006).

10. Richard Lau, Lee Sigelman, and Ivy Brown Rovner, "The Effects of Negative Political Advertisements: A Meta-Analytic Reassessment," *Journal of Politics* 69 (2007): 1176–1209.

11. "Study: Americans Roundly Reject Tailored Political Advertising as Politicians Embrace It," Annenberg School for Communication, University of Pennsylvania, press release, July 23, 2012, https://www.asc.upenn.edu/news-events /press-releases/study-americans-roundly-reject-tailored-political-advertising -politicians.

12. Erika Franklin Fowler, Michael M. Franz, and Travis N. Ridout, "Which Ads Persuade? Identifying Persuasive Characteristics in Political Advertising" (presentation, 11th Annual American Political Science Association Pre-Conference on Political Communication, Chicago, IL, August 2013); E. Franklin Fowler, P. Marshal Lawler, Michael Linden, Eliza Loomis, Zachary Wulderk, and Laura Baum, "A Messenger Like Me: The Effect of Average Spokespeople in Campaign Advertising," *Social Science Research Network,* September 3, 2014, http://papers.ssrn.com/abstract=2453472.

13. Fowler, Franz, and Ridout, "Which Ads Persuade?."

14. Patricia Strach, Katherine Zuber, Erika Franklin Fowler, Travis N. Ridout, and Kathleen Searles, "In a Different Voice? Explaining the Use of Men and Women as Voice-Over Announcers in Political Advertising," *Political Communication* 32, no. 2 (2015): 183–205.

15. Strach et al., "In a Different Voice?."

16. Eitan D. Hersh and Brian F. Schaffner, "Targeted Campaign Appeals and the Value of Ambiguity," *Journal of Politics* 75, no. 2 (April 2013): 520–534, doi: 10.1017/S0022381613000182.

17. Seth J. Hill, James Lo, Lynn Vavreck, and John Zaller, "How Quickly We Forget: The Duration of Persuasion Effects from Mass Communication," *Political Communication* 30, no. 4 (October 1, 2013): 521–547, doi:10.1080/10584609.2013.8 28143; Alan S. Gerber, James G. Gimpel, Donald P. Green, and Daron R. Shaw, "How Large and Long-Lasting Are the Persuasive Effects of Televised Campaign Ads? Results from a Randomized Field Experiment," *American Political Science Review* 105, no. 1 (February 2011): 135–150.

18. Hill et al., "How Quickly We Forget."

19. Travis N. Ridout and Michael M. Franz, *The Persuasive Power of Campaign Advertising* (Philadelphia, PA: Temple University Press, 2011).

20. Philip Rucker and Dan Balz, "How Joni Ernst's Ad about 'Castrating Hogs' Transformed Iowa's U.S. Senate Race," *Washington Post*, May 11, 2014, http://www.washingtonpost.com/politics/how-joni-ernsts-ad-about-castrating -hogs-transformed-iowas-us-senate-race/2014/05/11/c02d1804-d85b-11e3-95d3 -3bcd77cd4e11_story.html.

21. Erika Franklin Fowler and Travis N. Ridout, "Local Television and Newspaper Coverage of Advertising," *Political Communication* 26 (2009): 119–136; Patterson and McClure, *The Unseeing Eye*; James T. Hamilton, *All the News That's Fit to Sell: How the Market Transforms Information into News* (Princeton, NJ: Princeton University Press, 2004).

22. Fowler and Ridout, "Local Television and Newspaper Coverage of Advertising"; Travis N. Ridout and Glen R. Smith, "Free Advertising: How the Media Amplify Campaign Messages," *Political Research Quarterly* 61 (2008): 598–608.

23. Fowler and Ridout, "Local Television and Newspaper Coverage of Advertising."

24. Travis N. Ridout and Erika Franklin Fowler, "Explaining Perceptions of Advertising Tone," *Political Research Quarterly* 65, no. 1 (2012): 62–75.

25. Stephen Ansolabehere and Shanto Iyengar, *Going Negative: How Political Advertisements Shrink and Polarize the Electorate* (New York: Free Press, 1996); M. Pfau and A. Louden, "Effectiveness of Adwatch Formats in Deflecting Political Attack Ads," *Communication Research* 21, no. 3 (1994): 325–341.

26. Brendan Nyhan and Jason Reifler, "The Effect of Fact-Checking on Elites: A Field Experiment on U.S. State Legislators," *American Journal of Political Science* 59, no. 3 (July 2015): 628–640.

27. D. Stevens, "Measuring Exposure to Political Advertising in Surveys," *Political Behavior* 30, no. 1 (2008): 47–72.

28. Note, also, that our approach in Figure 7.2 for presidential ads is impossible for House and Senate races, where the campaign stops at the state or district border.

29. Christopher Weber, Johanna Dunaway, and Tyler Johnson, "It's All in the Name: Source Cue Ambiguity and the Persuasive Appeal of Campaign Ads," *Political Behavior* 34, no. 3 (September 1, 2012): 561–584, doi:10.1007/s11109-011-9172-y; Conor M. Dowling and Amber Wichowsky, "Attacks Without Consequence? Candidates, Parties, Groups, and the Changing Face of Negative Advertising," *American Journal of Political Science* 59, no. 1 (2015):19–36.

30. David W. Nickerson, "Is Voting Contagious? Evidence from Two Field Experiments," *American Political Science Review* 102 (February 2008): 49–57.

31. Costas Panagopoulos and Donald Green, "Field Experiments Testing the Impact of Radio Advertisements on Electoral Competition," *American Journal of Political Science* 52, no. 1 (2008): 156–168.

32. Derek Willis, "Professors' Research Project Stirs Political Outrage in Montana," The Upshot (blog), *New York Times*, October 28, 2014, http://www.nytimes.com/2014/10/29/upshot/professors-research-project-stirs-political-outrage-in-montana.html.

33. Thomas J. Leeper, "In Defense of the Montana Experiment," Thomas J. Leeper (blog), October 25, 2014, http://thomasleeper.com/2014/10/montana -experiment/.

CHAPTER 8

The Unintended Effects of Advertising

In the previous chapter we discussed the intended effects of advertising—its ability to persuade and to influence people's votes. In this chapter, we consider some of the *unintended* effects of advertising and whether or not they are good or bad for American society and democracy. Campaign managers and candidates may not think too much about this issue, but political scientists do. In this chapter, we will examine some of the questions political scientists have asked about the unintended effects of political advertising. For instance, what, if anything, do citizens learn from political advertising? How does watching a campaign season's worth of advertising influence people's perceptions of the tone of the race and their trust in government and politicians? And does exposure to political advertising have any impact on people's likelihood of participating in the political process—whether turning out to vote on Election Day or chatting with a friend about an election?

It is easy to dismiss political advertising as something damaging to American democracy, and if that is indeed the case, then citizens should be searching out ways to mitigate these harmful effects—and lobbying the government to do something about the problem. But before going down that road, citizens should be armed with data on the effects of advertising. While it would be naive to argue that political advertising is an unmitigated positive, we suggest—based on an assessment of the studies in the field on the subject—that the potential negative effects of advertising are overblown and there may even be some positive effects for society as a whole, including voter education.

WHAT DO WE LEARN FROM ADVERTISING?

What can people learn from political advertising? Your initial response might be, "Not much." After all, aren't political ads filled with lies? Not necessarily. Certainly, candidates do what they can to put themselves in the best possible light and to cast their opponents in the worst possible light, but that is the art of politics as it has been practiced for thousands of years, and it does not mean that they are lying. Although it is difficult to develop a neutral standard in politics for whether a claim is truthful or not, there are several factors that help prevent outright lies in political advertising. First, television stations are reluctant to air ads that are clearly false because they open themselves up to defamation lawsuits from the candidate attacked in the ad. Thus, advertisers are typically quite careful in trying to document the claims that they make. Indeed, 61 percent of the US Senate ads aired in 2014 cited some source to bolster the claims made in the ad, whether a newspaper article, a congressional bill, a website, or some other source.

Another factor that curbs false claims in advertising is **adwatch coverage**. As noted in Chapter 7, adwatch coverage occurs when the news media closely examine the claims made in ads and call out claims they deem false. An instance of this occurred during the 2012 presidential campaign when the Romney camp placed an ad on the air that asserted, "Obama took GM and Chrysler into bankruptcy and sold Chrysler to Italians who are going to build Jeeps in China."[1] The ad left the impression that Chrysler was closing factories in the US and shifting production to China. In fact, Chrysler was considering adding production in China, but not closing any US factories. Importantly, though, the news media called out the Romney campaign and attempted to correct the false impression. This Jeep ad example illustrates that while political advertising can sometimes be misleading, false claims are rare enough that they draw substantial media push-back. In addition, when the news media criticize an ad as untruthful, the ad's opponent often uses the media's language in his or her own advertising to attack the initial ad sponsor for "going negative" or "being misleading." In short, sponsors rarely get away with saying whatever they want, and there are enough deterrents—lawsuit threats, adwatch coverage, and accusations of "going negative"—to make a campaign think twice about telling outright lies.

Even though ads are not filled with lies, there is still the question of how much policy-oriented information one can glean from a typical thirty-second-long ad. Certainly, one stereotype of political advertising is that it includes little more than personal attacks. You have heard them all before: this candidate accepts money from Washington lobbyists, that candidate does not share our values. Just how much substantive, policy-based information is in a typical political ad?

We classified all House and Senate ads aired during the 2014 campaign into four categories: (1) mostly about policy matters (for example, education, crime, taxes); (2) mostly about candidates' personal characteristics; (3) about both policy and candidates; or (4) about neither (for example, an exhortation to vote on Election Day). As you can see in Table 8.1, the largest percentage of ads by far were focused on policy matters (60 percent). All told, 85 percent of ads made some mention of a policy issue—that's a significant amount of content for voters to learn from. Indeed, viewers may get a much greater proportion of issue content from political advertising than from news reports. A study of *New York Times* campaign coverage across thirteen presidential elections found that only one-quarter of total campaign-related coverage was focused on policy issues; the rest talked about the character of the candidates or the "horse race"—who is leading and who is trailing.[2]

Interestingly, ad sponsors are more likely to talk about policy when they are attacking another candidate than when they are promoting themselves or their favored candidates, as Table 8.2 shows. In 2014, 52 percent of positive ads were mostly concerned with policy matters, while 60 percent of contrast ads and 67 percent of negative ads were mostly concerned with policy. In some ways, this makes sense.

Table 8.1: Policy Focus in Advertising for Congressional Races, 2014

Policy matters	60.0%
Personal characteristics	13.0%
Both	25.0%
Neither	1.9%

Source: Wesleyan Media Project

Table 8.2: Policy Focus in Advertising by Ad Tone, Congressional Races, 2014

	Positive	Contrast	Negative
Policy matters	52.2%	60.3%	67.3%
Personal characteristics	16.3%	9.9%	11.5%
Both	28.5%	28.9%	19.8%
Neither	3.0%	0.8%	1.5%

Source: Wesleyan Media Project

Positive ads, especially early in a campaign, are often biographical. We learn that the candidate is experienced, has an adoring family, loves this country, and shares our values. But we are less likely to hear the candidate talk about his or her stance on the issues of the day. After all, taking a clear position on an issue can put you at odds with at least some percentage of voters who disagree. But when on the attack, it makes more sense for candidates to demonstrate to voters that their opponents' issue positions (unlike their own) are out of step with what the voters want.

Still, one might say that the amount of policy information conveyed in an ad is fairly minimal. There is a big difference between a candidate saying she wants to "improve health care" and a candidate saying she wants to "implement a single-payer health care system." The second statement provides information that is far more useful to the voter in deciding between candidates. How often, then, do ads provide more than just a general mention of a policy issue?

Table 8.3: Percentages of Policy-Based Ads Using Specific and General Frames

	Specific frame	General frame
Health care	94.9%	5.1%
Education	86.5%	13.5%
Taxes	79.2%	20.8%
Social Security	65.9%	34.1%

Percentages based on ads for US Senate in 2000, 2004, 2008, and 2012. *Source:* Wesleyan Media Project with analysis by the authors

Table 8.3 shows the percentage of ads across several campaign years that mention four different issues in a general fashion versus the percentage of ads that provide specifics about those same issues. For instance, if a candidate states a desire to "improve health care," "focus on education," or "reduce taxes," the candidate is using a general frame. But if the candidate states a desire to "protect a patient's choice of doctor," "increase local control of education," or "reduce payroll taxes," the candidate is using a specific frame. Though it varies by issue, there is a lot more specificity in ads than one might expect. On the issue of health care, for instance, only 5 percent of ads used a general frame; for education, it was 13.5 percent. For taxes, the use of general frames increased to about 21 percent. For Social Security, 34.1 percent of mentions were general. In sum, when ads sponsors talk about policy issues, they typically mention more than a mere desire for improvement; they offer some details that should enable voters to learn something useful about the candidates and their positions.

Of course, even when a candidate (or another ad sponsor) mentions an issue in a very general fashion, that still provides some information to voters. Repeatedly mentioning a desire to reduce crime—something almost everyone can agree with—can send a signal that the candidate will make that issue a priority if elected. And if you think crime is an important issue, knowing that a certain candidate will focus on the reduction of crime is highly useful information, especially given that politicians, after they are elected, tend to devote more time to those issues they talked about more on the campaign trail.[3]

Political advertising supplies considerable policy-specific information—more than one might expect—and thus there's a real possibility for voters to learn something from political advertising. But in addition to providing substantive information, there are some other ways by which political advertising could lead to learning. One is causing people to pay more attention to other political information. Let's say you see an ad promoting the presidential candidacy of Florida senator Marco Rubio. This may make you more interested in learning more about Rubio—you might be less likely to skip an article about Rubio when you see his name in the headline, or you may even decide to visit Rubio's website. In short, political advertising in this instance led to more interest, more name recognition, and more information-seeking—it led you to other sources from which you gathered information.

Another possible effect of political advertising is that it may help you draw inferences about a candidate's positions on issues. Perhaps you have seen the ad from 2014 Iowa Senate candidate Joni Ernst in which she was pictured in a firing range. The voiceover announcer started by noting, "She is not your typical candidate. Conservative Joni Ernst. Mom, farm girl, and lieutenant colonel who carries more than just lipstick in her purse." Much like Ernst's "Squeal" ad, which we discussed in the previous chapter, this ad cleverly used gun-related words and phrases to convey her positions. In particular, the voiceover mentioned that "she will take aim at wasteful spending" before Ernst appeared on-screen asking voters to "give [her] a shot."[4] The ad never mentioned her position on gun control. Still, you might (correctly) infer, given the imagery and word choice in the ad, that she is a strong defender of the Second Amendment right to bear arms. In short, although the ad focused on Ernst's opposition to government waste and Obamacare, the use of the gun, the setting of the firing range, and the wordplay were clearly chosen to articulate her position on the unrelated issue of gun rights (Figure 8.1).

Figure 8.1: Joni Ernst's 2014 "Shot" Ad for Senate

Source: Courtesy of Joni Ernst for U.S. Senate

Although there are many reasons voters might learn from political advertising, do voters actually learn something? To make this case, we turn to some other published research. One study matched up survey data about the types of television programs that people watched with data about the political ads airing where those people lived.[5] This allowed the authors to create a relative measure of ad exposure: people who watched many television programs during which many ads aired scored high, while those who watched little television or watched programs during which few ads aired scored low. The authors then compared people's exposure to ads aired in congressional races with their ability to recall accurately the names of their district's congressional candidates and found that more exposure led to better recall. They also compared people's exposure to ads airing in the presidential race in the year 2000 with their ability to correctly place candidate Al Gore to the left of candidate George W. Bush on an issue placement scale. Again, greater exposure to advertising was associated with a greater likelihood of correctly placing the candidates.

In another study, researchers used a similar procedure to compare exposure to political ads with knowledge about presidential candidates George W. Bush and Al Gore in the year 2000.[6] Four survey questions inquired about facts that appeared in the candidates' advertising, such as which candidate favored drilling for oil in Alaska's Arctic National Wildlife Refuge and which candidate favored allowing young people to devote up to one-sixth of their Social Security taxes to individually controlled investment accounts. Four questions asked about facts that did not appear in the candidates' advertising, such as which candidate had a brother who was a state governor and which candidate favored a seventy-two-hour waiting period for gun purchases at gun shows. Respondents who had been exposed to more advertising about the presidential campaign were able to answer correctly more of the questions about facts that appeared in advertising, but exposure to more advertising had no impact on people's ability to answer correctly questions about facts that did not appear in the advertising. Here, then, is pretty convincing evidence that people are learning facts from advertising that may be useful when casting their ballots.

We do not want to take this argument too far. Political advertising should not be voters' only source of information, but the ability of advertising to facilitate learning is far greater than one might think. Most political advertising has some policy content. Often that policy content contains enough specifics that voters can at least get a sense of how the candidate might address the issues, and even when the issue is mentioned generally (or even just implied, as gun rights is in the Ernst ad), it can reveal a candidate's priorities. Advertising may also spur people to seek out information from other sources and help them draw inferences about candidates' positions. An apt analogy is suggested by one set of researchers, who describe political ads as multivitamins: they cannot be one's only source of nutrition, but they can be effective supplements to other sources of information when it comes to learning about candidates.[7]

DO WE ACCURATELY PERCEIVE ADVERTISING AND CAMPAIGN TONE?

Campaign advertising can certainly be important in imparting knowledge about a candidate to voters, but it also may influence their broader impressions of the candidate's campaign. Citizens invariably complain about the negativity in campaign ads, and their impression of a campaign's advertising extends to the campaign as a whole. Yet there is a lot of variation across races and across candidates in the percentage of ads that are negative. To what extent, then, do citizens correctly perceive differences in negativity based on actual variation in the tone of races and between candidates?

At least one piece of research suggests that there is little correspondence between advertising tone and citizens' perceptions of the tone of the campaign.[8] In a study examining how much perceptions of the tone of a gubernatorial campaign varied across residents of the state, researchers found little agreement among citizens in whether the campaign was positive, negative, or mixed. This suggests that citizens' perceptions of tone are independent from the actual tone of advertising (at least as measured by scholars). Another explanation for this disconnect, however, could be that although residents of the state can vote for the same gubernatorial candidates, they may not necessarily be exposed to the same advertising messages. In previous chapters, we discussed how advertising can be targeted to particular audiences in particular locations and with particular television viewing habits. Advertising in a gubernatorial race in Pennsylvania may look a lot different in the media markets in the western half of the state, which is more conservative, than it does elsewhere, in part because of strategically placed advertising. In addition, differing television habits could also drive differences in how citizens perceive the tone of the race if, for example, a candidate chose to air positive ads during daytime soaps but went with more negative ads during news programming, which draws more politically sophisticated viewers. If the retired professor watches television during the daytime, she may legitimately have a different perception of the tone of the race than the office worker who arrives home just in time to catch the national news.

More recent research that accounts for some of these factors has found a stronger connection between advertising tone and perceptions of negativity. One study demonstrated that negativity in ads is a good predictor of the public's perceptions of campaign negativity.[9] Some have even shown that small amounts of positive advertising do decrease citizen perceptions of negativity—perhaps in part because positive ads may stand out against a background of negativity.[10] Yet the actual tone of advertising explains only a small percentage of the variation among citizens' perceptions of campaign tone. Other factors that influence this include one's partisanship. For example, a Republican is more likely than a Democrat to view a Democratic candidate's ads as negative while a Democrat is more likely than a Republican to view a Republican candidate's ads as negative. There is even evidence to suggest that women may perceive a particular campaign as more negative than men do.[11]

Finally, although citizens are exposed directly to campaign advertising, they also read and view news stories discussing advertising and the tone of the race, which can independently affect perceptions of the race. Reporters tend to focus on and amplify negative advertising in their coverage,[12] but they also tend to cover advertising through the lens of strategy, highlighting the tactics of the campaigns. Research suggests that media coverage of the strategy involved in advertising has an independent influence on citizen perceptions of ad tone.[13] In other words, after taking into account the actual tone of advertising and the demographic characteristics of viewers, the more citizens encounter discussions in the news about the tactical use of advertising, the more likely they are to view a candidate's advertising as negative. This finding may result from people's tendency to view politicians more cynically when politics is described as a game.

Another factor that may contribute to the disconnect between the actual tone of advertising aired and citizens' perceptions of the tone of advertising is that citizens do not always distinguish between ads sponsored by candidates and ads sponsored by parties or organized interests. As party and interest-group advertising both tend to be more negative than candidate airings, it is possible that citizens include ads they encounter by these other ad sponsors when assessing how negative a candidate has been.

Ultimately, we believe it is a good thing when citizens can accurately perceive the tone of a race. If citizens assume that candidates and other ad sponsors are highly negative—even when they are not—campaigns may run even more negative ads. After all, why be positive if voters do not recognize your "good behavior"? Likewise, we would not want a campaign in which voters are naively optimistic, assuming that politicians are engaging in positive advertising. In order to hold politicians accountable for their behaviors—whether you think negative advertising is good or bad—citizens must accurately perceive the tone of ads that those politicians are airing.

DOES ADVERTISING AFFECT OUR TRUST IN THE POLITICAL SYSTEM?

Turn on a television during an election season and you are almost certainly going to see some ads in which candidates are attacking each other—or groups are attacking candidates. And even when the ad is a "positive" one—that is, it does not mention a specific opponent—it may attack "politicians in Washington" or "government bureaucrats" or "special interest groups." Not surprisingly, some posit that greater exposure to political advertising could make a person less trusting of, and more cynical about, government and politicians.[14] It certainly seems logical that seeing a bunch of ads where politicians say negative things about each other might make people feel this way.

We know from previous chapters that the number of ads that contain attacks is high. Over 70 percent of the ads aired in US House and Senate races in 2014 mentioned an opponent.[15] Moreover, appeals to cynicism are common in political advertising. In 2008, 41 percent of the ads that aired in Senate races contained an appeal to cynicism.[16] Most often that cynicism was directed toward the opposing candidate, but sometimes it was directed toward government or Washington. For instance, Senate candidate Dave Cuddy from Alaska stated in his ad, "As long as we keep the folks in Washington from messing it up for us, Alaska's future is bright." In Louisiana, Senate candidate John Neely

Kennedy was even more direct, arguing, "Washington's in the ditch. It's broken. Now, let me be blunt. I am sick of the spending. I am sick of the waste. We will never change the culture of Washington by sending the same people back up there. If you want to change the Senate, you have to change the senator."[17]

In short, there is a lot in political advertising that could make one distrust the government and politicians and be cynical about their motives. And yet there are also reasons to doubt that exposure to political ads has this effect. For one, Americans have come to expect politicians to attack each other in political ads in October of an election year, so seeing such attacks is not out of the ordinary. Second, survey data support the idea that people are accepting of certain kinds of negative advertising—attacks that they deem legitimate and fair.[18] Most viewers believe that mentioning the other candidate is fair if the ad is talking about that person's issue positions or qualifications for office. Such ads are more effective than ads that viewers deem as unfair or illegitimate, like those that engage in **mudslinging**, personal attacks on a candidate's character or life.[19] Viewers also tend to get angry when ads become defamatory, like those that bring up a candidate's religion or family.[20] A good example of a defamatory ad that backfired is the one aired by Senate candidate Elizabeth Dole in North Carolina in 2008 that twisted the fact that the head of Godless Americans PAC held a fundraiser for Dole's opponent, Kay Hagan, into the charge that Hagan was an atheist. The ad even ended with an unidentified female voice saying, "There is no God!"[21] Hagan used Dole's ad as an opportunity to air her own ad on the topic, accusing Dole of "bearing false witness against fellow Christians."[22] In addition to drawing substantial negative coverage of Dole, the ad boosted support for Hagan by about five percentage points, according to Hagan's pollster.[23] Another good example of a defamatory ad that backfired comes from the 2010 Senate race in Kentucky; Jack Conway accused opponent Rand Paul of being a member of a "secret society that called the Holy Bible a hoax."[24] Polls taken the week after the ad aired showed that the percentage of Kentuckians disapproving of Conway jumped dramatically, and 69 percent believed the ad went too far.[25] Even if exposure to negative attacks and cynical appeals does reduce trust and increase feelings of cynicism, those effects may be fleeting. Once the ads disappear after Election Day, the negative feelings toward the government and politicians could slowly become more positive.

Overall, the best research in political science and communication supports the idea that advertising does not have any long-lasting negative effects on citizens' trust in the government and politicians. One study matched up survey data on people's attitudes toward the government with their viewing habits and the volume of negative ads that aired where they lived.[26] The study found absolutely no relationship between the amount of exposure people had to negative advertising and the following:

1. their approval of Congress
2. their perceptions of Congress's performance
3. their approval of Democratic leaders in Congress
4. their approval of Republican leaders in Congress
5. their feelings of internal efficacy (feeling that they can make a difference)
6. their feelings of external efficacy (feeling that the political system is responsive to them)

Other research, using a similar approach, even hints that increased exposure to political advertising (regardless of whether it is positive or negative) can increase trust in the government and weaken beliefs that elections need to be reformed and that money decides elections.[27] This may be because advertising—in which candidates ask citizens for their votes—reminds people that they, the voters, are ultimately in control.

Taken as a whole, then, political advertising seems not to have ill effects on people's trust in politicians and the government. Still, there may be particular types of advertising that result in a more negative reaction. One study found that voters are more than willing to accept political disagreement as a natural part of the political process, but their trust in the government starts to wane when that disagreement

Table 8.4: Perceived Fairness of Campaign Accusations

Accusation	Percent calling "fair" or "somewhat fair"
Talking one way and voting another	80.7
His/her voting record	75.8
His/her business practices	71.0
Taking money from special interest groups	70.7
Taking money from individuals with ethical problems	63.0
Current personal troubles	56.1
Current extramarital affairs	45.1
Political actions of his/her party's leaders	37.1
Past extramarital affairs	27.8
Past personal troubles	25.9
Personal lives of his/her party's leaders	19.1
Behavior of his/her family members	7.7

Data from 1999 Survey on Campaign Conduct, sponsored by the Thomas C. Sorensen Institute for Political Leadership. Paul Freedman, Dale Lawton, and Thomas M. Guterbock.

turns into incivility.[28] In 1999, the University of Virginia's Survey on Campaign Conduct[29] asked a random sample of Americans whether accusing an opponent of several campaign behaviors was fair game or not. The vast majority of people—at least 70 percent—said it was "fair" or "somewhat fair" to criticize an opponent for "talking one way and voting another," to criticize an opponent's voting record or business practices, or to mention an opponent taking money from special interest groups (see Table 8.4). But when the accusation gets more personal, people are less likely to agree it is fair. Only one in four Americans believes that past personal troubles are fair game, 19 percent believe that the personal lives of party leaders are fair, and only 7.7 percent agree that it is fair to bring up the behavior of a candidate's family members during a campaign. Thus, advertising may only have a negative impact on citizens' trust in the government and its efficacy when the advertisement is deemed uncivil, unfair, or irrelevant. Such ads are rare; in a typical election year, fewer than 2 percent of ads are uncivil.

DOES ADVERTISING INFLUENCE OUR POLITICAL PARTICIPATION?

Given the dominance of negativity on the airwaves during elections, the public's strong dislike of negativity, and the low voter turnout rates in the United States relative to many other democracies, it might seem natural to suggest that negative advertising is responsible for the fact that millions of Americans stay home on Election Day. In fact, some political scientists have argued just that: that negativity demobilizes the public.[30]

One explanation for this relationship is that citizens detest campaign attacks and therefore do not want to be associated with a system that is characterized by so much negativity, and thus they are not compelled to get out and vote. Another explanation could be that because negative ads decrease the favorability of the attacked candidate, enthusiasm for voting for that candidate decreases as well. Since both candidates in a competitive race tend to be the target of negativity, it stands to reason that citizens exposed to these negative attacks believe much of what they hear and decide that they don't want to vote for either candidate. Even if citizens do not necessarily believe the negative messages they encounter, they can still become upset with their favored candidate for getting down in the gutter and airing attacks against an opponent. This backlash, which we previously discussed as a central component of persuasion, may lead to decreased willingness to put the effort into showing up on Election Day to support their favored candidate.

Other scholars have questioned the idea that negativity decreases voter turnout,[31] and some have even argued that negativity may incite people to show up at the polls.[32] As we noted previously, negativity is more memorable than positivity, and citizens may learn more from negative ads because they have more substantive policy content,[33] all of which decreases the costs of acquiring information and makes it more likely that people will vote. Negativity that appeals to anger can also incite people's passions and convince them to take action. In fact, negativity in advertising may provide a stark contrast between the candidates, which also helps to convey that something important is at stake and that every vote is an important one.[34]

Perhaps no ad has conveyed the turnout stakes so clearly as the infamous "Daisy Girl" ad from the 1964 presidential campaign, which we first mentioned in Chapter 4. Recall that the ad, which was sponsored by incumbent Lyndon B. Johnson's campaign, showed a little girl in a meadow picking the petals off a daisy as she counts. When she reached nine, her voice was replaced by an authoritative male voice, which counted down as one would for a rocket launch. The camera zoomed in on the pupil in the little girl's eye, and when the countdown reached zero, images of a nuclear explosion filled the screen. The tagline of the ad stated explicitly: "Vote for President Johnson on November 3rd. The stakes are too high for you to stay home."[35] In part due to its controversial nature, the ad was aired only once by the campaign; however, news programs rebroadcast the ad numerous times in their coverage of the controversy. A more recent example of an ad that raises the stakes aired in the Arkansas Senate race in 2014. The ad, from Democrat Mark Pryor, featured news reports of the Ebola outbreak in Africa, noting that Pryor's Republican opponent, Tom Cotton, voted against preparing Americans for pandemics.[36]

Perhaps few other topics in advertising have garnered as much attention or as much debate as the effect of negativity on turnout. In fact, dozens of studies have attempted to speak to this question. Why so much focus on the relationship between campaign tone and turnout? One answer is that it is highly concerning for the health of the United States as a democracy if the conduct of campaigns is leading people to stay home on Election Day. Second, assessing the effect of negativity on participation has proven to be particularly difficult. Part of the reason for this is that the competitiveness of a race is associated with both increases in negativity and increases in mobilization; therefore, it is difficult to be sure that negativity on its own increases mobilization.

Some of the disagreement between scholars is also because different research methods tend to give different answers to the question.

Notably, the first scholars to argue that negativity was demobilizing relied primarily (though not exclusively) on the experimental method, which we described in Chapter 7. But scholars who have pursued observational research, in which they match up people's exposure to advertising in the real world with their reported turnout, have tended to find either no link between negativity and turnout or a positive relationship between the two. The most recent overview of scholarship on the link between negativity and turnout—which takes into account both experimental and observational studies—concluded that, overall, the effect of negative ads on turnout is no different than the effect of positive ads on turnout.[37] Of course, as we just discussed, not all negativity is equal. There is some evidence that mudslinging in advertising could be demobilizing, at least among a subset of the public, suggesting that different types of negativity may have different effects on turnout.[38]

Building upon arguments from those from both sides of the debate, scholar Yanna Krupnikov argues that negativity can both mobilize *and* demobilize, depending upon when a citizen encounters it.[39] Suppose you have not yet decided which candidate you are going to vote for. You turn on the television and see an ad suggesting that the candidate you were leaning towards voted for tax hikes on middle-class American families like yours. The ad highlights the candidate's ties to Washington and says she's not right for office. This concerns you, and so you seek out additional information. In short, the ad has gotten you to engage more in the process. However, let's say that after seeking out additional information, you determine that the ad's claims were overstated and you decide that you are indeed going to vote for that candidate because you have learned that she supports business development and you dislike her opponent's stance on education. A few days later, however, while watching your favorite prime time program, you see a new ad attacking your favored candidate, and it cites a newspaper you trust as evidence that her business development plan is poor and may result in more taxes on middle-class Americans. This new information doesn't make you want to vote for the opposing candidate—after all, you really disliked his education plan. But it does make you less enthusiastic about turning out to vote for your chosen candidate. As you can see from this example, seeing a negative ad after having made a candidate choice may demobilize while seeing a negative ad prior to having made a decision may mobilize.

CONCLUSION

This chapter has considered several unintended effects of political advertising, taking stock of scholarly evidence that speaks to several claims that have been made about advertising. We argued that people can learn from political ads, which often focus on policy issues and provide at least some specific indication of candidates' positions on those issues. We also noted that people can, in a broad sense, accurately report the tone of a political campaign, which helps them keep candidates accountable for the types of campaigns that they run. One complicating factor, though, is the fact that the news media tend to disproportionately cover negative advertising and that people may not be able to distinguish between candidates and groups as the source of campaign negativity.

In addition, exposure to advertising, even negative advertising, appears to have few negative impacts on people's trust in the government or politicians. Particularly uncivil attacks may start to erode that trust, but this type of attack is relatively rare. Finally, negative advertising, on average, has no real impact on levels of voter turnout, though certain individuals may be more inclined to stay home depending on the harshness of the advertising and the timing of the negativity. But those who stay home may be offset by those who are mobilized by seeing negative ads.

When it comes to political advertising, people tend to assume the worst: that advertising has no issue content, that it is full of lies, that it turns people off to politics and leads them to avoid the ballot box on Election Day. Yet a careful examination of the existing scholarly evidence about the unintended effects of political advertising paints a much different picture. At the very least, advertising does not have the negative effects that citizens, journalists, and sometimes even scholars attribute to it. What is the reason for this disconnect? We believe it may have to do with what comes to mind when people think about political advertising generally or negative political advertising in particular. Instead of thinking about positive biographical ads or ads that criticize an opponent's issue stands and governing priorities, citizens tend to think of the worst of the worst: mudslinging defamatory ads, such as the Elizabeth Dole ad from North Carolina. And when journalists talk about the problem of negativity, they use the most egregious examples, like ads that attack a candidate's child or mention her divorce. But the run-of-the-mill ads seen on television every day are something that most voters can live with, even if they can't embrace them.

DISCUSSION QUESTIONS

1. Citizens tend to think that advertising—especially negative advertising—has many ill effects on voters. And yet most scholarly research finds only very limited evidence of this. Why is there such a disconnect between what citizens and scholars believe? Are there explanations beyond what we offered in the conclusion?

2. Can you think of any political ads from recent campaigns that strike you as potentially damaging to viewers? How so? Is your conclusion consistent with the evidence presented in this chapter?

3. Are there changes that the news media should make in their coverage of advertising? Why do you believe these changes are warranted?

4. List three reasons why negative advertising might improve voter turnout. Provide an example of an ad aired in a real campaign that illustrates each of these reasons.

NOTES

1. Glenn Kessler, "4 Pinocchios for Mitt Romney's Misleading Ad on Chrysler and China," *Washington Post*, October 30, 2012, http://www.washingtonpost

.com/blogs/fact-checker/post/4-pinocchios-for-mitt-romneys-misleading-ad
-on-chrysler-and-china/2012/10/29/2a153a04-21d7-11e2-ac85-e669876c6a24_blog
.html.

2. William L. Benoit, Kevin A. Stein, and Glenn J. Hansen, "*New York Times*
Coverage of Presidential Campaigns," *Journalism & Mass Communication Quarterly* 82, no. 2 (2005): 356–376.

3. Michele P. Claibourn, *Presidential Campaigns and Presidential Accountability* (Champaign, IL: University of Illinois Press, 2011).

4. Maeve Reston, "Joni's June Event: Bikes and a Pig Roast," *CNN*, January 9,
2015, http://www.cnn.com/2015/01/09/politics/joni-ernst-roast-ride/.

5. Paul Freedman, Michael Franz, and Kenneth Goldstein, "Campaign Advertising and Democratic Citizenship," *American Journal of Political Science* 48, no.
4 (2004): 723–741.

6. Travis N. Ridout, Dhavan V. Shah, Kenneth M. Goldstein, and Michael M.
Franz, "Evaluating Measures of Campaign Advertising Exposure on Political
Learning," *Political Behavior* 26, no. 3 (2004): 201–225.

7. Michael M. Franz, Paul B. Freedman, Kenneth M. Goldstein, and Travis
N. Ridout, *Campaign Advertising and American Democracy* (Philadelphia, PA:
Temple University Press, 2007).

8. Lee Sigelman and Mark Kugler, "Why Is Research on the Effects of Negative
Campaigning So Inconclusive? Understanding Citizens' Perceptions of Negativity," *Journal of Politics* 65 (2003): 142–160.

9. John Sides, Keenz Lipsitz, Matthew Grossman, and Christine Trost, "Candidate Attacks and Voter Aversion: The Uncertain Effects of Negative Campaigning" (working paper, University of California-Berkeley, 2005); Travis N. Ridout
and Erika Franklin Fowler, "Explaining Perceptions of Advertising Tone," *Political Research Quarterly* 65, no. 1 (2012): 62–75; Kyle Mattes and David P. Redlawsk,
The Positive Case for Negative Advertising (Chicago, IL: University of Chicago
Press, 2014).

10. Ridout and Fowler, "Explaining Perceptions of Advertising Tone."

11. Sides et al., "Candidate Attacks and Voter Aversion."

12. Travis N. Ridout and Glen R. Smith, "Free Advertising: How the Media
Amplify Campaign Messages," *Political Research Quarterly* 61 (2008): 598–608;
Erika Franklin Fowler and Travis N. Ridout, "Local Television and Newspaper
Coverage of Political Advertising," *Political Communication* 26 (2009): 119–136.

13. Ridout and Fowler, "Explaining Perceptions of Advertising Tone."

14. Joseph N. Cappella and Kathleen Hall Jamieson, *Spiral of Cynicism: The
Press and the Public Good* (New York: Oxford University Press, 1997).

15. Erika Franklin Fowler and Travis N. Ridout, "Political Advertising in 2014:
The Year of the Outside Group," *The Forum: A Journal of Applied Research in
Contemporary Politics* 12, no. 4 (2014): 663–684.

16. Sanne Rijkhoff and Travis N. Ridout, "Your Lying, Incompetent and Self-ish Member of Congress: Cynical Appeals in U.S. Senate Advertising" (working paper, Washington State University, 2015).

17. Storyboards for these two ads are archived at the Wisconsin Advertising Project (http://wiscadproject.wisc.edu/). The Cuddy ad first aired February 29, 2008, while the Kennedy ad first aired September 5, 2008.

18. Mattes and Redlawsk, *The Positive Case for Negative Campaigning*.

19. Kim Leslie Fridkin and Patrick J. Kenney, "Do Negative Messages Work? The Impact of Negativity on Citizens' Evaluations of Candidates," *American Politics Research* 32 (2004): 570–605.

20. Mattes and Redlawsk, *The Positive Case for Negative Campaigning*.

21. "Dole Challenger Irate over Suggestion She Is 'Godless,'" *CNN*, October 30, 2008, http://edition.cnn.com/2008/POLITICS/10/30/dole.ad/.

22. Paul Kane, "Rival Is Church Official: Sen. Dole Makes Issue of 'Godless' Group," *Washington Post*, October 31, 2008, http://www.washingtonpost.com/wp-dyn/content/article/2008/10/30/AR2008103004432.html.

23. Josh Kraushaar, "Hagan Pollster: 'Godless' Ad Backfired, Big Time," *Politico*, November 10, 2008, http://www.politico.com/blogs/scorecard/1108/Hagan_pollster_Godless_ad_backfired_big_time.html.

24. Gregory Korte. "Conway Ad in Ky. Questions Rand Paul's Beliefs," *USA Today*, October 19, 2010, http://usatoday30.usatoday.com/news/politics/2010-10-19-adwatch19_ST_N.htm.

25. Manu Raju, "'Aqua Buddha' Ad Backfires," *Politico*, October 26, 2010, http://www.politico.com/story/2010/10/aqua-buddha-ad-backfires-044222.

26. Robert A. Jackson, Jeffery J. Mondak, and Robert Huckfeldt, "Examining the Possible Corrosive Impact of Negative Advertising on Citizens' Attitudes Toward Politics," *Political Research Quarterly* 62, no. 1 (March 2009): 55–69.

27. Franz et al., *Campaign Advertising and American Democracy*.

28. Diana C. Mutz and Byron Reeves, "The New Videomalaise: Effects of Tele-vised Incivility on Political Trust," *American Political Science Review* 99, no. 1 (2005): 1–15.

29. Paul Freedman, Dale Lawton, and Thomas M. Guterbock, "Survey on Campaign Conduct: Preliminary Report of Results," Thomas C. Sorensen Institute for Political Leadership, http://www.virginia.edu/surveys/press/scc-report.pdf.

30. Stephen Ansolabehere and Shanto Iyengar, *Going Negative: How Political Advertisements Shrink and Polarize the Electorate* (New York: Free Press, 1996).

31. Steven E. Finkel and John G. Geer, "A Spot Check: Casting Doubt on the Demobilizing Effect of Attack Advertising," *American Journal of Political Science* 42, no. 2 (1998): 573–595; Joshua D. Clinton and John S. Lapinski, "'Targeted' Advertising and Voter Turnout: An Experimental Study of the 2000 Presidential

Election," *Journal of Politics* 66, no. 1 (2004): 69–96; Jonathan S. Krasno and Donald P. Green, "Do Televised Presidential Ads Increase Voter Turnout? Evidence from a Natural Experiment," *Journal of Politics* 70, no. 1 (2008): 245–261.

32. Paul Freedman and Ken Goldstein, "Measuring Media Exposure and the Effects of Negative Campaign Ads," *American Journal of Political Science* 43, no. 4 (1999): 1189–1208; Franz et al., *Campaign Advertising and American Democracy.*

33. John G. Geer, *In Defense of Negativity: Attack Ads in Presidential Campaigns* (Chicago: University of Chicago Press, 2006); but see Daniel Stevens, "Tone Versus Information: Explaining the Impact of Negative Political Advertising," *Journal of Political Marketing* 11, no. 4 (2012): 322–352. Stevens notes that the beneficial effects of negative ads may be due primarily to the increased information provided rather than their tone.

34. Paul A. Djupe and David A. M. Peterson, "The Impact of Negative Campaigning: Evidence from the 1998 Senatorial Primaries," *Political Research Quarterly* 55 (2002): 845–860; Franz et al., *Campaign Advertising and American Democracy.*

35. Wisconsin Advertising Project, Historic Ad Archive, http://wiscadproject.wisc.edu/history.php.

36. https://www.youtube.com/watch?v=c8xYDfwqNWk.

37. Richard R. Lau, Lee Sigelman, and Ivy Brown Rovner, "The Effects of Negative Political Campaigns: A Meta-Analytic Reassessment," *Journal of Politics* 69, no. 4 (2007): 1176–1209.

38. Kim Fridkin Kahn and Patrick J. Kenney, "Do Negative Campaigns Mobilize or Suppress Turnout? Clarifying the Relationship Between Negativity and Participation," *American Political Science Review* 93, no. 4 (1999): 877–889.

39. Yanna Krupnikov, "When Does Negativity Demobilize? Tracing the Conditional Effect of Negative Campaigning on Voter Turnout," *American Journal of Political Science* 55, no. 4 (2011): 797–813.

CHAPTER 9

The Future of Political Advertising and Its Role in Our Society

This book has discussed how political advertising is made and bought, how it is regulated, and what its effects are on citizens. But in this final chapter, we want to turn our eyes to the future and discuss how the use of political advertising may change and the potential consequences of those changes on campaigns, parties, interest groups, and—most importantly—the American public. We will focus, in particular, on technological change and changes in the regulation of political advertising. Finally, we will discuss the broader role of political advertising in the US political landscape and society.

TECHNOLOGICAL CHANGE

One technological change that has the potential to upend how political advertising is purchased, delivered, and tracked is addressable advertising, which we discussed briefly in Chapter 5. Distributors of advertising—whether cable, satellite, or streaming—will have the ability to vary the ad shown depending on the characteristics of the household. This will give ad sponsors the ability to show different ads in different homes—even if they are all on the same block. This capability already exists on satellite providers Dish Network and DirectTV and should soon be possible on major cable television providers, such as Comcast. In a sense, the purchase and distribution of television advertising is likely to become much more similar to the purchase and distribution of online advertising as discussed in Chapter 6.

As campaigns move substantial dollars to addressable advertising, there are several possible implications. One potential advantage of such a move is that it may allow campaigns to speak to issues that individuals are concerned about. If you are concerned about reproductive health issues, then receiving an ad about that issue from a candidate may be beneficial to you as a voter. Moreover, if you're nineteen, why should you have to hear an ad that talks about shoring up the Medicare program for senior citizens?

Yet there are some potential downsides of campaigns' moving en masse to addressable advertising. Some might argue that voters ultimately vote for candidates, not positions on one or two issues, and thus they should be exposed to the candidates' views on a wide variety of issues, not just the one they care about the most. A second concern is that the mandate to govern is much stronger when a campaign is about something, not dozens of things, and using a consistent message with all groups of voters can give a winning candidate the legitimacy needed to act. For example, a winning candidate will have difficulty claiming that the people want her to address climate change if she only talked about climate change with a small percentage of the electorate.

A third concern is accountability. Addressable television advertising might make it too easy for candidates to tell different types of voters exactly what they want to hear. Candidates should not be able to promise more agricultural subsidies to farmers and fewer agricultural subsidies to fiscal conservatives. Finally, tracking addressable television advertising will be difficult—it carries much the same types of technological challenges we face in tracking online advertising—leaving citizens, journalists, and even campaigns with potentially less information than they currently have about who is advertising and what those sponsors are saying.

Although we can sketch out many possible implications of the use of addressable television advertising, all of these depend on campaigns' having access to quality information. Yet recent research on microtargeting strategies employed in the "ground campaign" (for example, direct voter contact through door-to-door canvassing, phone calls, and direct mail), which draws on the actual databases used by practitioners, suggests that campaigns actually have less detailed and less accurate information on voters than is often assumed.[1] Importantly, as scholar Eitan Hersh argues, campaign strategies are built upon campaign *perceptions* of who voters are, based on the information they have about them in their databases, not necessarily the actual voter profiles with all their complexities. Addressable advertising is no different than these other ways of voter contact in that its success depends on access to high-quality, detailed information.

CHANGES IN REGULATION

In recent years, there has been a strong movement toward group-sponsored campaign advertising in the United States and a movement away from party-sponsored advertising. This change has resulted, in substantial part, from Supreme Court rulings that have made it easier for groups to raise money and spend money on electioneering activities. Yet it is uncertain whether this movement of ad dollars to groups will continue in 2016 and beyond.

Some prognosticators believe that groups will continue to raise and spend considerable dollars on advertising but the pace of growth will slow. Under one scenario, we may find groups heavily involved in television advertising during the early months of campaigns, when they do not necessarily need to disclose their activity and costs to advertise are lower, but turning over the bulk of advertising to candidates closer to Election Day. This division of labor would allow the candidates to pay the lowest unit rate (to which groups are not entitled) to television stations, leaving groups free to engage in ground efforts and online advertising.

Thus, donors may find giving money to candidates more attractive as it gives more "bang for the buck"—at least in the last couple of months of the campaign, when the "lowest unit rate" window kicks in. Giving money to candidates was also made slightly easier by the *McCutcheon v. Federal Election Commission* Supreme Court decision in 2014, which invalidated overall limits on how much individuals can give to candidates, parties, and traditional political action committees. At the same time, in late 2014 Congress raised the limit on how much donors can give to political parties for their conventions, legal fees, and building projects. Although that money may not be spent on advertising, it does give donors another potential outlet for their money and may mean fewer big checks are being written to groups.

Still, even with these developments, group-sponsored advertising promises to be huge well into the near future, given the lack of rules and rule enforcement. One concern is that a substantial chunk of this spending will continue to be dark money spending. About 35 percent of the ad spending by groups in House, Senate, and gubernatorial races in 2014 came from dark money groups—those that do not need to disclose their donors.[2] Thus, voters lack information that is useful in evaluating the truthfulness of the ad's message.

While there will surely continue to be dark money advertising in future election cycles, whether it increases as a share of total advertising is still an open question. While many donors like being able to give as much as they want without anyone knowing they are playing in electoral politics, some donors want the influence that comes with politicians knowing that you are spending big sums of money to support their election to office, and others don't care one way or the other. Either way, it is clear that citizens lack knowledge about even the largest groups that advertise on the air, let alone the numerous smaller groups that pop up to sponsor an ad in a particular race.

The rise of outside group advertising brings both challenges and opportunities for candidates. One challenge for candidates' campaigns is that groups may hijack the issue agenda by running ads about issues that candidates do not want to talk about. Most campaigns have thought out, well in advance, the themes they want to emphasize to voters each week of the campaign, even if they also try to remain agile in responses to their opponents. But well-laid plans to talk about education one week may be foiled if an outside group enters the race with a two-million-dollar ad buy that attacks an opponent for his failure to support Israel. Messages are no longer consistent, and voters may be confused. Sometimes, the last thing that candidates want is the "help" of an interest group.

On the other hand, it sometimes seems as though groups and candidates are working hand in hand, coordinating their election efforts. Right to Rise, a super PAC founded by supporters of Jeb Bush, is taking on many functions traditionally handled by candidates' campaigns.[3] Indeed, some suggest that Bush delayed his announcement as a candidate for the 2016 Republican presidential nomination precisely so that he could travel the country and raise money for the super PAC— something that would be prohibited if he were an official candidate. Here, then, is an instance in which a candidate's campaign, instead of being hijacked by a group, is outsourcing many activities to that group. The larger point is that the extent to which a group helps or hurts a candidate depends on the characteristics of the group, like whether it has its own ideological agenda, issue concerns, or membership base.[4] Groups with ideological agendas and members who care about issues are much more likely to inject their own issues into the race, while multi-issue groups without members are much more likely to echo what the candidates talk about.

The rise of groups also has potential impacts for political parties. A network of groups headed by the Koch brothers has announced plans to raise and spend almost nine hundred million dollars in the 2016 election cycle, much of it, presumably, on political advertising.[5] Given this dollar amount, it would not be surprising if the Koch brothers' network spends more than the Republican Party on advertising, an unwelcome prospect for those in the party's leadership. It could be the case, then, that loyalty to the Koch brothers and their ideological and issue positions becomes more important for a Republican candidate's success than loyalty to the Republican Party.

What is especially concerning, at least to some, is that contributors to these groups do not represent Americans but are a small slice of the extremely rich. Given the high cost of political advertising, only the rich can afford to become involved in campaigns. Consider this example from 2012. Winning Our Future, Republican presidential candidate Newt Gingrich's super PAC, received twenty million dollars in contributions from billionaire Sheldon Adelson. When Adelson has talked politics, it has generally been to argue that US policy toward Israel is too pro-Palestinian.[6] That Adelson is so associated with one issue engendered worries that if Newt Gingrich was elected president, his policy with regard to Israel would be unduly influenced—even dictated—by Adelson's hard-line views.

The continued presence, and possible growth, of group-sponsored advertising in campaigns may also have an impact on voters. For one, voters may have less knowledge overall of who is responsible for the ads they see on television. When the bulk of advertising came from candidates or parties, it was easy to identify the ad's sponsorship, especially in the case of candidates, who are required to announce who they are and that they approved the ad's message. And so voters knew whom to hold accountable for the ad's content: if you did not like what you saw, you could vote against the party or the candidate. And knowing that, say, Barack Obama or the Democratic Party sponsored an ad that attacked Mitt Romney is useful information in judging the truth behind those attacks. But when unknown groups with pleasant-sounding names like Patriot Majority (or even Americans for a More American America) sponsors the ad, voters have very little useful information with which to judge the ad. All that they know is that a group with a nice name does not like the candidate. What is even more concerning is that research has found that when the sponsor is an unknown group, the ad is even more effective than when a candidate sponsors it.[7]

Yet there is a potential upside to group sponsorship of advertising: it may be able to cut through polarization. When an ad is sponsored by a Republican candidate or the Republican Party, Democrats tend to tune it out. Likewise, when an ad is sponsored by a Democratic candidate or the Democratic Party, Republicans tend to tune it out. But when the ad is sponsored by, say, the American Unity PAC, both Republicans and Democrats may be more likely to listen to the ad's message, given that very few are likely to know that the American Unity PAC is, for the record, a conservative group.

BROADER IMPACTS OF POLITICAL ADVERTISING

Ultimately, then, is the role of political advertising in the United States a positive or negative one? That's a difficult question to answer, though we tend to be more positive about the role of advertising in contemporary campaigns than many others who study advertising or report on it in the news media. There is evidence that ads contain considerable policy-based information and that voters can learn from these ads. Ads can provide cues, like helping voters figure out whether the candidate is more liberal, moderate, or conservative, or motivating them to seek out additional information. There is also evidence that advertising can even stimulate political participation and seldom demobilizes voters. And when it comes to the idea that watching a bunch of political ads makes people persistently cynical about politics and politicians—well, there is scant evidence of that.

Still, many worry that political advertising—because of its slick visuals and emotional appeals—is manipulative, convincing people to vote for candidates who would not act in their best interest. While we have no doubt that ads can persuade voters, we find the claim that ads manipulate voters goes too far. For one, a single ad seldom airs in isolation. People are exposed to numerous individual ads—perhaps hundreds of times—over the course of a campaign. One particularly effective ad can be counteracted by an ad from the other side. Second, voters are often smarter than scholars give them credit for. As we argued in Chapter 8, campaigns seldom get away with bald-faced lies, and voters hold advertisers accountable when they cross a line, such as when they start talking about a candidate's family or religion. Third, although voters are not totally immune to messages from a candidate with whom they disagree,[8] their partisanship often provides an anchor that makes it difficult to move them from supporting their party. Instead of accepting the argument of a particularly compelling

Republican-sponsored ad, Democrats are more likely to question it, reinterpret it, or dismiss it. Finally, assuming it's a competitive race, most people who identify as Democrats end up voting for the Democratic candidate, and most people who identify as Republicans end up voting for the Republican candidate. And so, given all that we know, the idea that advertising manipulates is a bit too strong.

Potentially more worrisome is that the huge cost of television advertising gives undue influence to interests with a lot of cash—the "one percent," in contemporary lingo. In response, some might point out that Democrats have been able to effectively compete with Republicans in the political advertising game, in spite of the fact that Republicans are supposedly the party of big business. While Democrats generally do raise more of their money from small-dollar donors than Republicans, there are plenty of mega-rich donors giving to candidates in both parties. The problem, as many see it, is that the concerns of the working poor, the disabled, the undernourished, antiwar advocates, day laborers, and immigrants are not being expressed in campaign discourse because representatives of these groups do not have the millions of dollars necessary to play the advertising game. While it is true that campaigns feature "everyday Americans" in their ads, it is also the case that the rich and mega-rich have more access to politicians and more influence on the policies that come from Washington, DC. The optimistic response to this scenario is that the Internet has the ability to change this concentration of political power in the hands of the very rich. Maybe so. But the best evidence suggests that, at least up to this point, the Internet, instead of transforming campaign advertising, is just a new campaign platform for traditional political actors to use.

CONCLUSION

Political advertising is a billion-dollar business in the United States. It represents the largest expense for most campaigns, and since the advent of television, it has contributed to the skyrocketing costs of campaigning. Because of its centrality to successful campaigns, decisions about ad content and placement are taken very seriously. Advertising becomes fodder for a seemingly disproportionate amount of media attention, and scholars debate advertising's potential negative impacts on American democracy. Although there remains disagreement about the proper role of political advertising in the US, at the end of the day, there is one thing that almost everyone can agree on: advertising is an essential part of the entertaining spectacle that is the American political campaign.

DISCUSSION QUESTIONS

1. On the whole, do you believe that technological change in how political advertising is distributed will make it more or less relevant to campaigns in upcoming election cycles? Why or why not?

2. Assume that Congress passes regulations making it extremely difficult for outside groups to raise money to be spent on political advertising and thus money starts flowing back into the coffers of candidates and parties. What consequences would that have for how candidates run their campaigns? For the political parties? For voters?

3. In your view, what would the role of advertising be in an ideal campaign system? Would there be a lot, a little, or none? Who would pay for it? On which mediums would it appear?

NOTES

1. Eitan Hersh, *Hacking the Electorate* (Cambridge, UK: Cambridge University Press, 2015).

2. Erika Franklin Fowler and Travis N. Ridout, "Political Advertising in 2014: The Year of the Outside Group," *The Forum: A Journal of Applied Research in Contemporary Politics* 12, no. 4 (2014): 663–684.

3. Alex Isenstadt, "Jeb Bush's $100M May," *Politico,* May 8, 2015, http://www.politico.com/story/2015/05/jeb-bush-right-to-rise-super-pac-campaign-117753.html.

4. Michael M. Franz, Erika Franklin Fowler, and Travis N. Ridout, "Loose Cannons or Loyal Foot Soldiers? Toward a More Complex Theory of Interest Group Advertising Strategies," *American Journal of Political Science* (forthcoming).

5. Peter Overby, "Koch Brothers Rival GOP with Plans to Spend $900 Million in 2016," *All Things Considered,* NPR, January 27, 2015, http://www.npr.org/2015

/01/27/381942730/koch-brothers-rival-gop-with-plans-to-spend-900-million-in
-2016.

6. Molly Ball, "Who Is Sheldon Adelson, the Gingrich Super PAC's Billionaire
Backer?," *The Atlantic,* January 25, 2012, http://www.theatlantic.com/politics
/archive/2012/01/who-is-sheldon-adelson-the-gingrich-super-pacs-billionaire
-backer/252003/.

7. Deborah Jordan Brooks and Michael Murov, "Assessing Accountability in
a Post–*Citizens United* Era: The Effects of Attack Ad Sponsorship by Unknown
Independent Groups," *American Politics Research* 40, no. 3 (2012): 383–418; Travis
N. Ridout, Michael M. Franz, and Erika Franklin Fowler, "Sponsorship, Disclo-
sure, and Donors: Limiting the Impact of Outside Group Ads," *Political Research
Quarterly* 68, no. 1 (March 2015): 154–166.

8. Travis N. Ridout and Michael M. Franz, *The Persuasive Power of Campaign
Advertising* (Philadelphia, PA: Temple University Press, 2011).

Glossary

501c organization: Nonprofit group that can air political advertisements that advocate for or against federal candidates, as long as such activity is not the group's primary focus. These organizations do not have to publicly disclose their donors.

Ad amplification: Occurs when news media cover an ad extensively, giving it additional airtime without cost to the sponsor. Also known as *free advertising*.

Ad targeting: The practice of strategically placing ads to reach voters of different demographics. See also *microtargeting*.

Addressable advertising: A new type of televised advertising, currently available on satellite TV, in which the ads shown to viewers differ by household based on demographics.

Adwatch coverage: Media coverage that focuses on evaluating the accuracy of an advertisement's message.

Aggregate-level analysis: An analysis of data on groups of people rather than individuals.

Airing: One showing of an ad on television—on a particular day, at a particular time, in a particular media market. (Cf. *creative.*)

Backlash: When the sponsor of a negative ad suffers a decline in favorability after airing the ad.

Banner ad: A large advertisement that appears across a website (usually the top) and encourages viewers to click to see the advertised content.

Benchmark survey: An initial survey of voters that provides the campaign with information on how much (if anything) voters already know about the candidate and how they feel about particular issues and themes likely to be used in the campaign.

Bipartisan Campaign Reform Act (BCRA): Federal legislation passed in 2002 that outlawed the parties' use of soft money and forced the parties to use only regulated hard money for any and all expenditures. Also known as the Mc-Cain–Feingold Act.

B-roll video: Audio-free video footage, which is often used to produce political ads.

Buckley v. Valeo: The 1976 Supreme Court decision that invalidated some components of the Federal Election Campaign Act of 1974. It remains important today, particularly for a footnote that hypothesized that a set of magic words could be used to distinguish between issue advocacy, which can be paid for through soft money, and federal-level electioneering, which must be paid for by hard money.

Cable interconnects: Groups of local cable television systems that are linked together, allowing cable companies to easily insert ads between programs.

Candidate-sponsored advertising: Ads sponsored directly by candidates and paid for out of their own campaign accounts. These ads are uncoordinated with parties and groups.

Citizens United v. Federal Election Commission: The 2010 Supreme Court case in which five of the nine justices argued that restrictions on interest group electioneering were unconstitutional under the First Amendment.

Competitiveness ratings: Estimates of how close a race is likely to be, ranging from safe for one candidate to a toss-up.

Conditional effects theory: The notion that messages should not be expected to influence all citizens equally at all times and that their impact will vary depending on both the characteristics of the person who receives the message and the characteristics of the information environment. Also known as *heterogenous effects.*

Contrast ad: An ad that mentions both main candidates in a race. Typically, such ads promote one candidate in part of the ad and attack the opposing candidate in the remainder of the ad.

Coordinated advertising: Ads jointly sponsored and paid for by a candidate and party. There are strict limits on how much money a party can spend on such ads.

Creative: An ad made for television. Creatives may air on television a number of times. (Cf. *airing*.)

Cutting the cord: Dropping cable or satellite television service in favor of streaming video via an Internet connection to a computer, tablet, or television set.

Dark money: Funds used to pay for election campaign activities or political advertising that is spent by entities, such as 501c4s, 501c5s, and 501c6s, that do not publicly disclose their donors.

Daypart: Time of day during which television programming airs—for example, prime time, early morning, late night.

Dial testing: Form of ad testing in which participants use a dial to register positive or negative feelings toward components of an advertisement.

Display advertising: Online ads relying primarily on images, audio, and/or video to convey their messages.

Earned media: Media coverage of campaign events or campaign advertising that helps to spread its messaging.

Earned online media: The dissemination of campaign messages through social media users who watch and share videos, images, or other messages, post and "like" them on Facebook, or retweet them on Twitter. See also *earned media*.

Endogeneity: In statistics, when a variable is determined by other variables within a system; because the variables likely affect each other, this makes it difficult to confirm causation.

Experiments: A form of research allowing the researcher to control who experiences the treatment and who does not.

Exposure: The extent to which a citizen is likely to have encountered a particular message; being in the presence of the message.

Express advocacy: Advertising that explicitly endorses the election or defeat of a candidate. Typically, these are messages that contain so-called *magic words*.

Federal Communications Commission (FCC): The government agency that regulates broadcast media, including television and radio.

Federal Election Campaign Act (FECA): The major campaign finance reform bill, passed in 1971 and revised and expanded in 1974, that states that candidates can only accept contributions from individual citizens, party committees, and political action committees (PACs), banning them from accepting direct contributions from corporations and unions. It also limited party and PAC contributions to candidates and established the Federal Election Commission.

Federal Election Commission (FEC): The government agency that regulates the financing of federal campaigns and to whom campaigns, parties, and PACs have to report their fund-raising and expenditures.

Field experiment: A form of research that combines randomization with observational tracking in the real world.

Focus groups: Gatherings of small groups of people (typically seven to twelve) who engage in a conversation guided by a moderator about a particular topic. Focus groups are often used for advertising testing.

Gross ratings point (GRP): A unit of measurement that gauges the reach of an advertising campaign. One GRP is equal to 1 percent of the potential targeted audience.

Hard money: Funds collected within the limits prescribed by law on the size of contributions from individuals, parties, and PACs and used directly for federal elections.

Horserace coverage: Media coverage of an election that is focused on which candidate is winning or losing a race and which side is winning or losing a debate.

Hypodermic needle theory: A theory that posits that messages can be injected into the public in such a way that they are automatically accepted and spread throughout society.

Independent expenditure: Spending aimed at helping a candidate that is not coordinated with the candidate's campaign.

Individual-level analysis: The analysis of information on specific individuals and their attitudes and opinions about advertising and/or the candidates.

Interest-group advertising: Ads sponsored by an interest group, not a candidate or party.

Issue advocacy: Advertising that does not explicitly endorse the election or defeat of a candidate but instead focuses, at least in theory, on promoting certain values and ideas. These are ads that might depict or feature a candidate but do not include *magic words*.

Issue convergence: A measure of how much overlap there is between sponsors on the issues mentioned in ads. Two sponsors whose ads talk about entirely different sets of issues would have no issue convergence.

Knowledge gap: The growing discrepancy in knowledge between political novices, who don't intentionally follow politics, and political sophisticates, who do.

Level of analysis: An indication of whether data are observed and recorded in terms of individuals or in terms of groups of people.

Local cable television: Programming (usually in the form of advertising) on national cable networks that is seen only in particular cities or even neighborhoods.

Lowest unit rate: The rule established by the 1971 Federal Election Campaign Act that states that forty-five days before a primary and sixty days before a general election, broadcasters must sell advertising time to candidates at the cheapest price available for the requested time.

Magic words: Key words listed in a footnote of *Buckley v. Valeo* that the court suggested could be used to determine whether an interest group or party advertisement could be paid for by hard or soft money. Specifically, if an ad used any of the following words, it should be paid for by hard money: "vote for," "elect," "support," "cast your ballot for," "[Smith] for Congress," "vote against," "defeat," or "reject." (See also *express advocacy* and *issue advocacy*.)

Media market: A region in which the population receives similar television and radio stations. Also known as a *designated market area (DMA)*.

Microtargeting: The process of using available data to locate specific partisans for get-out-the vote messages and/or specific independents or opposing partisans for persuasion messages.

Minimal effects model: The theory that mass media had little impact on the public due to strong predispositions and selective exposure.

Mudslinging: Personal attacks on a candidate's character or family, which citizens typically view as unfair.

National broadcast television: Television that airs everywhere in the country on one of the major broadcast networks, which can be viewed without a cable subscription.

National cable network: A television channel, such as HGTV, CNN, ESPN, or Lifetime, that requires a cable subscription but can be viewed nationally.

Negative ad: An ad that speaks only about a candidate opposed by the ad's sponsor.

Network affiliate: A local television station that broadcasts a particular network's programs.

Observational approach: A research method that involves observing and measuring real-world factors and then statistically controlling for factors believed to be related to the outcome of interest.

Online acquisition: Campaign efforts to obtain individual voter contact information—e-mail or mailing addresses and phone numbers—so they can continue to solicit action and donations throughout the campaign. Sometimes also called *direct response.*

Paid online media: Campaign efforts to reach audiences by purchasing advertising on social media platforms.

Panel data: Survey data in which researchers track the opinions of individual voters over time.

Party-sponsored advertising: Ads paid for by political parties.

Political action committee (PAC): An association of individuals affiliated with corporations, unions, or trade associations whose members pool their own money into a common pot, which is distributed to candidates (within the limits established in FECA) as campaign contributions.

Political novices: Those who pay little attention to politics and do not seek out information about it.

Political sophisticates: Those who spend time thinking about political information and have firmer preexisting attitudes as a result.

Positive ad: An ad that speaks only about the candidate favored by the ad's sponsor.

Predispositions: Preexisting opinions and political views, including partisan attachments.

Pre-roll ad: An ad that appears before viewers watch an unrelated YouTube video or see content on a website.

Prime time: Evening daypart (eight to eleven p.m. on the East and West Coasts and seven to ten p.m. Central/Mountain time) during which the largest audiences watching television are found.

Private-citizen advertising: Political ads paid for by everyday citizens. Such ads are extremely rare.

Programmatic advertising: Automatic processing of real-time bids from campaigns for online advertising space based on preset parameters.

Randomization: A process that ensures that each participant in an experiment has an equal chance of being assigned to the treatment or control group.

Remarketing: Advertising based on prior online actions, such as visiting a website or searching for a candidate, where viewers have not yet taken a specific action (like donating money or signing up to receive e-mails).

Search advertising: Type of advertising purchased by campaigns that is tailored to your online search behavior.

Selective exposure: The pursuit of information that confirms predispositions and/or avoidance of information that contradicts them.

Social media: Online platforms that allow individuals to create and share content as well as view and comment on other users' content, whether text, images, or video.

Soft money: Money raised outside the regulated system of federal campaign finance laws from otherwise prohibited sources, such as corporations and unions.

Spot: One airing of an advertisement.

Super PAC: Group that can accept and spend unlimited amounts of money but must fully report its contributors and how much they gave, as well as all expenditures by the Super PAC, to the Federal Election Commission.

Targeting analysis: Survey assessment of which voters already support a candidate and who among the electorate can be persuaded.

Two-sided information flows: Message environment in which competing campaigns actively vie for citizen attention through equally matched advertising volumes.

Index

CPSIA information can be obtained at www.ICGtesting.com
Printed in the USA
LVOW10s1119090816

499638LV00012B/42/P